EXPLORING AMORIS LAETITIA

⁕

Exploring
Amoris
Laetitia

Opening the Pope's Love Letter to Families

EDITED BY BREDA O'BRIEN

VERITAS

Published 2017 by Veritas Publications
7–8 Lower Abbey Street
Dublin 1, Ireland
publications@veritas.ie
www.veritas.ie

ISBN 978 1 84730 784 2

10 9 8 7 6 5 4 3 2 1

A catalogue record for this book is available from the British Library.

Cover designed by Heather Costello, Veritas Publications
Printed in the Republic of Ireland by SPRINT-print Ltd, Dublin

*Veritas books are printed on paper made from the wood pulp of managed
forests. For every tree felled, at least one tree is planted, thereby renewing
natural resources.*

Contents

Foreword

In *Familiaris Consortio*, Saint John Paul II wrote that the, 'future of humanity passes by way of the family' (*FC*, 86). This laconic statement contains an insight and wisdom about which we need to be reminded often to ensure that our care of the family is a key priority for the Church and for society. Moreover the 'future of humanity' is something that touches our identity, our aspirations, and our commitment to what God wishes for human beings and for the world, something revealed most eloquently throughout the Scriptures.

In *Evangelii Gaudium*, Pope Francis observed that, 'the family is the fundamental cell of society, where we learn to live with others despite our differences and to belong to one another; it is also the place where parents pass on the faith to their children' (*EG*, 66). Surely the many challenges faced by our world – and indeed our country – would be made less fraught, less tense, if we could learn to live with and belong to each other; and surely the family as the special locus for the transmission of faith means that this handing on of faith within the family is something profoundly sacred.

When Pope Francis convened an Extraordinary General Assembly of the Synod of Bishops for 2014, followed by a General Assembly for 2015, it was clear that he, with his long experience as a pastor, was underlining the importance of our support for marriage and the family. *Amoris Laetitia* is the fruit of Pope Francis' reflections following these meetings of the Synod of Bishops. As a participant in this assembly, which met during 2015, I was privileged to witness the sharing of perspectives and experiences as bishops from all over the world grappled with the great social, economic, theological and cultural questions faced by families. I was also conscious of the need to articulate the Church's beautiful richness of teaching and pastoral care for families in a way that is Christ-centred and credible for the men, women and children of our time.

I warmly welcome the publication of *Exploring Amoris Laetitia* as another lens through which to read and ruminate on the hidden gems contained in the text of Pope Francis, not in an attempt to bypass reading *Amoris Laetitia* but in order to plumb its riches. This book of essays is also timely as we prepare for the ninth World Meeting of Families in Dublin in August 2018, the holding of which Pope Francis has already expressly linked to, 'the teaching of *Amoris Laetitia*, with which the Church wishes families always to be in step, in that inner pilgrimage that is the manifestation of authentic life'.[1] My prayer is that as a result of our exploration of *Amoris Laetitia*, the 'Gospel of the Family' will be at the centre of our proclamation of and witness to the Jesus Christ who is the 'way, the truth and the life' (Jn 14:6).

✠ Archbishop Eamon Martin

---

1. Letter of His Holiness Pope Francis on the occasion of the ninth World Meeting of Families on the Theme: 'The Gospel of the Family: Joy to the World' (25 March 2017)

Introduction

Amoris Laetitia was published during the Extraordinary Jubilee of Mercy, which Pope Francis suggested was particularly appropriate for two reasons:

> First, because it represents an invitation to Christian families to value the gifts of marriage and the family, and to persevere in a love strengthened by the virtues of generosity, commitment, fidelity and patience. Second, because it seeks to encourage everyone to be a sign of mercy and closeness wherever family life remains imperfect or lacks peace and joy. (*AL*, 5)

These two reasons apply with equal validity to the preparation for the World Meeting of Families in 2018. Each world meeting is not just an event: it represents a vital opportunity for the Christian community to reflect on and renew itself. This book is designed to help small groups to begin to look more closely at *Amoris Laetitia*, not as a substitute for the exhortation itself, but as a way of beginning to study that accessible – if long – document.

Each contributor was asked to focus on a particular chapter of *Amoris Laetitia* and to write about it in the light of his or own insights and experience. Although this book could be profitably read by an individual seeking insights into the papal exhortation, it might work best as the basis for a small group study course where a chapter is assigned every week or fortnight, and people meet to discuss it in a parish or home setting, or even in an online group. Individual chapters could also be read and discussed by pastoral councils or other initiatives within a parish; it may, for instance, be of use for those who work with young families during sacramental preparation.

Each section has questions designed to help participants deepen and broaden their understanding of the vocation to married and family life, so that they are encouraged to bear witness to that vision in every facet of their everyday lives.

Breda O'Brien

Chapter One
In the Light of the Word
BISHOP BRENDAN LEAHY

The Bible is full of Love Stories and Family Crises

At the 2015 Synod of Bishops on the vocation and mission of
the family, Archbishop Diarmuid Martin stated that 'simply
repeating doctrinal formulations alone will not bring the Gospel
and the Good News of the family into an antagonistic society'.
He pointed out that we need to find a language that can be a
bridge to the day-to-day reality of marriage. Pope Francis also
acknowledges that there is a difficulty. The Church's message
about the family can often seem to lack compassion or simply be
too abstract. While recognising the great value of the teachings
on family and marriage that are part of the Church's treasure
trove, Pope Francis invites us to learn again how to present
the Gospel of the family, reminding us that the Bible 'is full
of families, births, love stories and family crises' (*AL,* 8). He
wants us to make the Bible's realism our own. The Bible leads
us to contemplate both the dream – that is, the ideal picture
of the family according to God's loving plan – as well as the
'bitter truth found throughout sacred Scripture, that is, the
presence of pain, evil and violence that break up families and
their communion of life and love' (*AL,* 19). When we realise the
Word of God 'is not a series of abstract ideas but rather a source
of comfort and companionship for every family that experiences
difficulties or suffering' (*AL,* 22), we come to see that the Word
of God encourages us to, in the words of the title of chapter
eight, 'accompany, discern and integrate weakness' in family life.

For the Jesuit Pope, our engagement with the Word of God
is central. The Word of God guides discernment. It allows our

minds, hearts and wills to be shaped by God's tone and vision. It frees us of rigidity in facing reality. Pope Francis refers to the Bible many times in the exhortation. While chapter one is explicitly dedicated to the Word of God, the reader will also benefit greatly from a careful reading of chapter four's sustained contemplation on love in marriage based on 1 Corinthians 13. This meditative treatment of the famous passage on love, read so often at weddings, is unparalleled in magisterial documents.

Seeing Life in the Light of the Word

Pope Francis frames his meditation on the Word of God in chapter one by a repeated reference to Psalm 128. This is a psalm that features in the Jewish wedding liturgy and is also sometimes found in Christian wedding liturgies. So straightaway, we are brought to the wedding day, the day of dreams, hopes and new beginnings. The Pope then invites us to 'cross the threshold' of the home and hear the stories of love that feature in family life.

In the first instance, he invites us to reflect on the couple, the father and mother 'with their personal story of love'. As the Book of Genesis and the history of salvation indicate, the couple is a 'living icon' that reveals God. Their fruitful love becomes a symbol of God's inner life. Their love for one another images nothing less than the mystery of the Triune God, 'for, in the Christian vision of the Trinity, God is contemplated as Father, Son and Spirit of love. The triune God is a communion of love ...' (*AL*, 11)

In reflecting on love in the family, the love of the couple has a certain primacy that can never be forgotten. At a funeral ceremony that I attended recently, the son of the deceased spoke at the graveside saying, 'My father and mother gave us many things in life, but above all, the example of their love for one another'. Pope Francis would rejoice at this comment because he emphasises that the portrait of a couple delineated in Scripture is of a face-to-face encounter, marked by self-giving in love. As Scripture indicates, the marital union has many dimensions – sexual, corporeal and self-giving love. The woman of the Song of Songs expresses this with her declaration, 'My beloved is mine and I am his … I am my beloved and my beloved is mine' (Song 2: 16; 6:3). In his Letter to the Ephesians, St Paul links the husband–wife relationship to the 'mystery' of the union of Christ and the Church (Eph 5:21-33).

From the joy of a couple's love, Pope Francis moves to a reflection on the children, full of energy and vitality. He writes, 'If the parents are in some sense the foundations of the home, the children are like the "living stones" of the family' (cf. 1 Pet 2:5) (*AL*, 14). It is moving to note Pope Francis' reading of Jesus' attitude to children. In Jesus' time, the society of the ancient Near East did not view children as having particular rights. They were considered to be family property. From Jesus, however, we learn to respect that children have their own lives to lead. They make serious life decisions. Indeed Jesus goes so far as to present children as teachers: 'Truly I say to you, unless you turn and become like children, you will never enter the kingdom of heaven. Whoever humbles himself like this child, he is the greatest in the kingdom of heaven' (Mt 18: 3-4).

Pope Francis invites us then to consider 'the living space of the family'. The family images the communion of life in God: 'The word of God tells us that the family is entrusted to a man, a woman and their children, so that they may become a communion of persons in the image of the union of the Father, the Son and the Holy Spirit' (*AL*, 29). Saint John Paul II is quoted as saying that God 'is not solitude but a family'.

Speaking at the World Gathering of Families in Philadelphia in September 2015, Pope Francis remarked that in the Garden of Eden, all the love God has in himself, all the beauty God has in himself, all the truth God has in himself, he entrusted to the family. And in his typically homely imagery, he commented that:

> The family has a divine identity card. Do you see what I mean? God gave the family an identity card so that families could be places in our world where his truth, love and beauty could continue to take root and grow.[1]

From Scripture we know that in the early Church, 'a family's living space could turn into a domestic church, a setting for the Eucharist, the presence of Christ seated at its table' (*AL,* 15). The family is the place where children are brought up in the faith. It is a place of craftsmanship, where children learn the family 'trade' (*AL,* 16), a task to be carried out with tenderness (*AL,* 28).

A moving example of learning the family 'trade' comes from a tragic situation during the war in Bosnia some years ago. When fighting broke out in a certain area, some children were sent away to a safe place where they remained for some time. When told it was safe to return, they did so only to discover their village reduced to a shell, their father lying dead and their mother inside the house, crushed by suffering. Others arrived with the suspected murderer. All that was necessary was for the mother to condemn him; the children pleaded with her to do so. But she would not, replying, 'All of you played together when you were children. Your father and I always taught you to forgive. Now comes our moment to really forgive and not condemn.' Initially, the children could not understand their mother's reaction but gradually came to realise the mother's heroism and learned from it. They learned to forgive.

Having presented many positive aspects of the family as depicted in Scripture, Pope Francis goes on to indicate how Scripture also bears witness to the path of suffering that people can experience in marriage and family life. The very opening pages of the Bible tell us about Cain's murder of his brother Abel. The Bible then continues to speak to us 'of the disputes between the sons and wives of the patriarchs Abraham, Isaac and Jacob ... the tragedies and violence marking the family of David, the family problems reflected in the story of Tobias ...' (*AL*, 20). In a particularly striking short summary, Pope Francis reminds us of how much Jesus himself knew the dimensions of suffering in family life:

> Jesus himself was born into a modest family that soon
> had to flee to a foreign land. He visits the home of Peter,
> whose mother-in-law is ill (cf. Mk 1:30-31) and shows
> sympathy upon hearing of deaths in the homes of Jairus
> and Lazarus (cf. Mk 5:22-24, 35-43; Jn 11:1-44). He
> hears the desperate wailing of the widow of Nain for
> her dead son (cf. Lk 7:11-15) and heeds the plea of the
> father of an epileptic child in a small country town (cf.
> Mk 9:17-27). He goes to the homes of tax collectors
> like Matthew and Zacchaeus (cf. Mt 9:9-13; Lk 19:1-
> 10) and speaks to sinners like the woman in the house
> of Simon the Pharisee (cf. Lk 7:36-50). Jesus knows
> the anxieties and tensions experienced by families and
> he weaves them into his parables: children who leave
> home to seek adventure (cf. Lk 15:11-32), or who prove
> troublesome (Mt 21:28-31) or fall prey to violence (Mk
> 12:1-9). He is also sensitive to the embarrassment caused

by the lack of wine at a wedding feast (Jn 2:1-10), the failure of guests to come to a banquet (Mt 22:1-10), and the anxiety of a poor family over the loss of a coin (Lk 15:8-10). (*AL*, 21)

Pope Francis acknowledges the many pressures on family life today. While 'begetting and raising children … mirrors God's creative work' (*AL*, 29), issues of unemployment, as well as 'the social degeneration' seen in social and economic imbalances denounced by the prophets, not to mention the ravaging of the earth, all impact negatively on family life.

Pope Francis refers us to the icon of the Holy Family of Nazareth. In an oft-quoted homily of 1964, Pope Paul VI too said that he would like to return to his childhood and attend the simple yet profound school that is Nazareth. But Pope Francis also notes 'its daily life had its share of burdens and even nightmares, as when they met with Herod's implacable violence', an experience that 'continues to afflict the many refugee families who in our day feel rejected and helpless' (*AL*, 30).

As the Bible indicates, in God's plan family life is meant to be made up of relationships of love and tenderness. But because of sin, these relationships can turn into dynamics of domination. It is only in following Jesus Christ's way of love that we find the key to living the journey of family life. He gives the measure of love: laying down one's life for others (cf. Jn 15:13) and love that 'bears fruit in mercy and forgiveness' (*AL*, 27).

The family is on a journey. During that journey, we can never presume or claim perfection in one another. One day the family will reach the goal of its journey and it is then that God 'will wipe away every tear from their eyes, and death shall be no more, neither shall there be mourning nor crying nor pain any more' (Rev 21:4 quoted in *AL*, 22). But for now, it is essential to always remember the journey dimension of family life. As Pope Francis writes towards the end of his exhortation, summarising his reading of Scripture and reflections in the light of the Synod discussions:

> No family drops down from heaven perfectly formed; families need constantly to grow and mature in the ability to love. This is a never-ending vocation born of the full communion of the Trinity … Our contemplation of the fulfilment which we have yet to attain also allows us to see in proper perspective the historical journey which we make as families, and in this way to stop demanding of our interpersonal relationships a perfection, a purity of intentions and a consistency which we will only encounter in the Kingdom to come. It also keeps us from judging harshly those who live in situations of frailty. (*AL,* 325)

In his concluding address at the 2015 Synod, Pope Francis quoted Pope Benedict, reminding us that mercy is the nucleus of the Gospel message. Mercy is always needed for the family journey.

The Family and the Word of God

Joy is one of the great themes of Pope Francis' pontificate. But that should never be confused with a superficial happiness. Life's circumstances and difficulties tell us as much. It is joy rooted in the Word of God that Pope Francis wants us to discover along life's journey. In his apostolic exhortation, *Evangelii Gaudium,* he writes, 'The joy of the Gospel fills the hearts and lives of all who encounter Jesus'. To nurture the joy of love in the family,

Pope Francis recognises 'the family is called ... to read the word of God' (*AL*, 29). The Bishops at the Synod affirmed: 'the word of God is the source of life and spirituality for the family' and 'the word of God is not only good news in a person's private life but also a criterion of judgement and a light in discerning the various challenges that married couples and families encounter' (*AL*, 227).

The family can profitably take up the explanation of how to engage with the Word of God that Pope Francis offers in *Evangelii Gaudium.*[2] In that document, he explains that:

> ... in the presence of God, during a recollected reading of the text, it is good to ask, for example: 'Lord, what does this text say to me? What is it about my life that you want to change by this text? What troubles me about this text? Why am I not interested in this? Or perhaps: What do I find pleasant in this text? What is it about this word that moves me? What attracts me? Why does it attract me?'

Of course, when we read the Gospel and try to put it into practice, certain temptations usually arise: 'One of them is simply to feel troubled or burdened and to turn away. Another common temptation is to think about what the text means for other people, and so avoid applying it to our own life. It can also happen that we look for excuses to water down the clear meaning of the text. Or we can wonder if God is demanding too much of us, asking for a decision which we are not yet prepared to make.' Even when we notice such temptations we should keep going. God is patient with us: 'He always invites us to take a step forward, but does not demand a full response if we are not yet ready. He simply asks that we sincerely look at our life and present ourselves honestly before him, and that we be willing to continue to grow, asking from him what we ourselves cannot as yet achieve'.

It is not without significance that many of the Church movements that have come to life in recent times, including those that focus on family, manifest a particular love for the Word of God. One movement gathers the children together every Sunday morning for a review of some of the biblical stories. Another movement encourages families to have a cube/dice of love with characteristics of the Gospel art of loving written on each side of the cube. Every day, they throw the dice and focus on living out that characteristic during the day. In the evening, or occasionally during the week, they take time out to share the experiences of the Gospel they have lived. Many families take a brief moment occasionally to read a short piece of Scripture at meal time. Many years ago, Pope Paul VI suggested to all the faithful to take one sentence from the Sunday Gospel and try to keep that as the focus for the week.

Conclusion

Amoris Laetitia is a wonderful document, one that is not to be read rapidly but contemplated and studied carefully. In reading it, the temptation might be to skim through the first chapter and flick on to later chapters that deal with more 'controversial' issues. But Pope Francis warns us against this. That would be akin to the mindless rush into the kind of debates that were carried on 'in the media, in certain publications and even among the Church's ministers' around the time of the Synods, debates that ranged from 'an immoderate desire for total change without sufficient reflection or grounding, to an attitude that would solve everything by applying general rules or deriving undue conclusions from particular theological considerations' (*AL*, 2).

In drawing up *Amoris Laetitia*, Pope Francis has not only listened to the discussions of two synods. He has also listened to what has been said around the world in documents of the bishops' conferences in Latin America, the Caribbean, Mexico, Kenya, Australia, Colombia, Italy, Korea, Spain and Chile. He also listened attentively to the teachings of Saint John Paul on the 'theology of the body' and the 'language of the body', to the Second Vatican Council's Pastoral Constitution on the Church in the Modern World, *Gaudium et Spes* as well as Pope Paul's encyclical *Humanae Vitae* and Pope Benedict XVI's *Deus Caritas*. He has also taken note of comments from authors such as Martin Luther King, Erich Fromm and Dietrich Bonhoeffer. And yet the basic text for Pope Francis is the Word of God. His hope is that families themselves, and all who are called to minister with and to families, will take the Word of God to heart and learn to reflect its message, its tone, and its educational style.

There can be little doubt that Pope Francis has been following a strong intuition or inspiration in focusing so powerfully on the theme of family and marriage from early on in his papacy. With the heart of a pastor, Pope Francis acknowledges, 'we also need to be humble and realistic, acknowledging that at times the way we present our Christian beliefs and treat other people has helped contribute to today's problematic situation' (*AL*, 36).

His great desire has been to discern well what God is calling the Church today to do in communicating the joy of love in the family. In *Amoris Laetitia*, Pope Francis issues an invitation to all of us – discover 'the Christian proclamation on the family is good news indeed' (*AL*, 1). Biblical realism is about dreaming God's dream for the family but also hearing God's story of accompaniment of families in fragile situations. It is this biblical realism that makes Pope Francis want to reach out to everyone (cf. *AL*, 297).

Reflection Questions

1. 'The Church's message about the family can often seem to lack compassion or simply be too abstract.' Is this an accurate statement? If so, what can be done to demonstrate that the message is both compassionate and concrete?

2. What might Pope Francis mean when he says: 'the family has a divine identity card'?

3. Consider the incident in Bosnia in which children offer forgiveness to someone suspected of killing their father. Can you think of other instances where 'learning the family trade' is difficult or challenging?

4. How might families integrate Scripture, the Word of God, into busy lives in ways that are age-appropriate for every family member?

Endnotes

1. World Meeting of Families, Philadelphia, 26 September 2015
2. Pope Francis' Apostolic Exhortation on the Joy of the Gospel, *Evangelii Gaudium*, n. 153

Chapter Two
The Experiences and Challenges of Families

BAIRBRE CAHILL

I have yet to meet a perfect family. As far as I know – and I include my own family in this – we all mess up to some degree. Some of the mess we create ourselves through living lives that are too busy or creating expectations that we cannot live up to. Some of the chaos comes upon us from forces in our society and our world. Family life can be a challenging path. Some of the more difficult of these challenges are highlighted by Pope Francis in chapter two of *Amoris Laetitia*. Indeed, we only have to watch the news to see evidence of what Pope Francis speaks about. We see refugees drowning in the Mediterranean, children dying in Syria, families homeless on the streets of our own cities, lives ravaged by drugs, adults and children enslaved to provide cheap labour or sexual pleasure. Each headline is about a person, a person who has had a life before chaos, a person who is not simply an isolated individual but is part of a larger family.

We need to be careful not to read those words of Pope Francis about challenges facing the family out of context. Even those involved in the second Synod on the Family warned of the dangers of focussing on the negatives instead of the positives of family life. For Pope Francis however, there is a need to ground our conversation about families in the reality of life – good and bad. Yes, family life can be challenging and even chaotic but family is also the place where most of us first encounter love and tenderness. Just think of a toddler giggling with his daddy or a family sitting around a dinner table or a mum wrapping her teenage daughter in a cuddle after a row. In the love of family we glimpse the love and mercy of God. God is encountered in the ordinary everyday of family life and so Pope Francis speaks about family as a community of love (*AL*, 11), speaks of the 'gospel of the family' (*AL*, 200) and the spirituality of family life.

The Family Is Good News

Let's explore that idea of the gospel of the family. What does that mean? It cannot only be the Gospel that is heard *by* the family. It also must mean that the family is a gospel, is good news, for itself, for others and for society. So, the gospel of the family is something living and active. As we have already realised, no family has a perfect life so this gospel must be something that survives and thrives even amidst the chaos, challenges and busyness of ordinary family life. This applies to families as we encounter them today. We know from experience that families come in all shapes and sizes. When we speak about the gospel of the family we are talking about families with lots of children and families with only one, about adoptive families and foster families, about families with marriage and families without marriage, single parents, guardians and grandparents parenting, about huge extended families and small families. Family is bigger than any single definition and whatever our family we all come with our strengths and our weaknesses. In all of this it is worth remembering the words which the monks of Taizé sing, '*Ubi caritas, Deus ibi est*' – where love exists God is present. A family's life may look chaotic from the outside but still be experienced within as a place of love where God is present and active. Pope Francis warns against producing a theology of the family which is artificial and disconnected from life (cf. *AL*, 36) so when he speaks of the gospel of the family this must be something down to earth, something we could all relate to. What is this gospel?

When I work with groups of parents whose children are preparing for sacraments I always tell them that their family home is one of the holiest places their child can be. That can sound like madness. I don't know about your family home but ours wouldn't strike anyone as your typical idea of a holy place! There are piles of clothes to be ironed, dishes to be dried, football boots and kit bags to be cleaned, a dog who seems to lose more hair every day than she has on her body, a fridge that mysteriously empties as soon as I do the shopping and endless debates and arguments about every topic under the sun!

So how can it make sense to talk about home as a holy place or about the gospel of the family? This is where we come to the idea of the spirituality of family life. Spirituality is not an add-on, something that we build up by the number of prayers we say or the holy pictures we have hanging on our walls. Ronald Rolheiser[1] talks about spirituality as the energy that fires us. It comes from the very core of who we are and finds expression in the way we live our life. So the spirituality of family life really means that there is something about the ordinary day-to-day reality of family life – with all its joys and challenges – that speaks to us about God. In amidst the school runs, meals cooked, stories read, homework checked, cuddles given, boundaries established and dreams nurtured we glimpse the face of God who created us and calls us to fullness of life. Family life is a place where we encounter God in the daily challenges to love, forgive, nurture and grow together in love – and that is why we can talk about the gospel of the family. It is when we tap into this reality of who we are that we, as family, can be counter-cultural, can challenge the individualistic, consumer-driven culture that causes so much pain and fragmentation in our society.

Our culture is obsessed with the freedom of the individual to make whatever choices he or she wants. This can lead to a mentality where all that matters is what gives me pleasure here and now. We could call this the pleasure principle and it is a very powerful thing if that is the energy which is directing our life and shaping our choices. As a mother, I certainly have days where I just want to escape, to please myself and do my own thing but I also know that family life cannot really function like that. Both marriage and family life put relationships centre stage. We are created for relationship. From birth we have a deep need and desire to be known, loved and understood. For a young child life is a journey of discovery, gradually learning that relationships work best when we love *and* are loved, when we give *and* take, when we speak *and* listen. We are learning what mutuality is about, what love is about. In this way we can say that the relationships of family life are an invitation into the very heart of God. Why? Loving relationship is the dynamic energy of the Trinity. The love between the Father and the Son overflows through the Holy Spirit. It is in this love that we, 'live and move and have our being' (Acts 17:28). As St John tells us (cf. 1 John 4) our ability to love is rooted in the fact that God first loved us.

Now, is all this beginning to sound idealistic, artificial, disconnected from the realities of family life? The love I have in mind is a very earthy, physical thing. This love is seen in the peeling of spuds and the baking of bread, in the cleaning up of cut knees and the cup of tea with a stressed-out teenager. It is seen in the hug of a sweaty boy coming home from training and the quiet moments of conversation snatched out of a busy day. This love is found in laughter and in tears, in the tenderness of touch and in the setting of boundaries and it proclaims to the world that relationships matter. We come to know ourselves most deeply not in isolation but in relationship with others.

I would go even further and say that this love is what Incarnation is about. The love in family is not an abstract idea. It is love made real, given shape and form in the bits and pieces of life. In Jesus the love of God was made real, physical, literally given flesh, which is what incarnation means. That means that people could encounter God in and through the humanity of Jesus. So because of Jesus, God is at the heart of our humanity and our humanity is at the heart of God. All those ways in family life that we show our love for each other – even when it is a struggle to do so – become ways of echoing God's love in the world. Family life becomes a celebration of the Incarnation, God with us. We become the ongoing face of God's love. Through Baptism we become part of the Body of Christ and in our loving we make Christ present in the world.

The Family As Sacrament

That is why it makes sense to talk about the sacramental reality of family life. We are used to talking about the sacraments of the Church. We are less accustomed to talking about the sacramental reality of everyday life. Calling something a sacrament means that we have absolute confidence that God is present. If our relationships invite us into the very heart of God and the love we live day in, day out echoes God's love then this is something sacred at the core of our lives as family. To speak about the sacramental reality of life is to say that here in our midst, God is present and active. If our lives are a place where we encounter God, then that challenges the notion that faith is just about practice. We can all fall into a way of thinking that divides life up into holy bits and ordinary bits. We might think of the church building as a place where God is present but not think of our homes in the same way. We might see the rituals of the Church as speaking to us about God but not realise that the patterns of our own lives and the created world also speak to us of God. The spirituality of family life challenges us to see all of life as a piece, faith and life flowing together, God as present as the air we breathe.

If we begin to glimpse the sacred reality at the heart of our lives then we realise the significance of what one popular advertisement calls, 'the wonderful everyday'. The meals that we share around the kitchen table are powerfully linked to what we celebrate in the Eucharist at Mass. Just look at the Gospels and notice how much time Jesus spent sharing meals with people. To be together, nurtured and strengthened by food and by the company of others – this is the stuff of holiness. For myself, it was in the experience of carrying, birthing and breastfeeding four children that I came to a new awareness of what Eucharist means. Those words, 'This is my body broken for you, this is my blood poured out for you' have taken on a whole new depth of meaning. Parents have a living understanding of what self-sacrificing love is all about – in big ways and in countless small silent acts of love. So, too, forgiveness begins in the home and shapes our understanding of the sacrament of reconciliation. Sacraments of healing take root in the kissing better of bumps and bruises. God's face is glimpsed in the love of family life.

Now don't get me wrong: I don't think any family is perfect or even anywhere close. There are days when I look at our own family and think, 'Well if this is my path to holiness I think I'm in bother!' We get things wrong, we make a mess, we can be selfish and angry and nasty. This too is part of the reality of family life and the reality of our humanity. We are all sometimes fragile, broken and scared. If our relationships matter to us then they will bring us not only joy but also pain. The challenge is to keep loving, beyond the hurt and despite our own brokenness.

This can be an experience of the Paschal Mystery where we glimpse something of Jesus' own suffering and death. If Jesus had loved God and us less surely he could have walked away from Jerusalem, avoided the cross, lived his own life? But the power of his love would not let him abandon us or betray God's message – and so he stayed and suffered and died. In family life we too pay the cost of loving. Growing beyond our own selfishness and the demands of our ego is a challenging but necessary experience in both marriage and family life. Seeing life from the perspective of others, developing empathy, learning tolerance and how to forgive and be forgiven are all essential skills. Some families are pushed further by the circumstances of life, experiencing the cross in a very real way through the pain of a broken relationship, abuse or addiction.

Many parents that I have worked with over the years have talked about their sense of responsibility and fear when their baby is placed in their arms for the first time. We have an almost overwhelming desire to protect this little one from harm which is tempered by the knowledge that we will not always be able to do that. Love makes us vulnerable. Allowing other fragile, mortal human beings to stand at the centre of our lives means we are liable to experience fear, suffering, grief and loss. What makes it worth taking the risk? Love – that is the most powerful reason why we allow ourselves to be so vulnerable. As Christians too, we are called to believe that because of Jesus' Resurrection, life and love are stronger than death. It can be hard to hold on to that hope and often it is the love and strength of family and friends that keep us strong. Hope is incarnate, given flesh, in the goodness of others.

Here in the midst of family life then is an invitation into the heart of God, an experience of Incarnation, an awareness of sacred reality and the presence of God. Here there is an encounter with fragility and suffering and a strength that can carry us through. Pope Francis speaks of the need in family life to be open to grace. What is grace if not the presence and action of God in our lives? Confidence that our lives, messy as they might be, are holy ground – this is what the gospel of the family is about.

So what, if anything, does this have to say to the challenges which Pope Francis highlights in chapter two of *Amoris Laetitia*? Pope Francis quotes from *Relatio Synodi* on this subject:

> 'On the other hand the growing danger represented by an extreme individualism which weakens family bonds and ends up considering each member of the family as an isolated unit, leading in some cases to the idea that one's personality is shaped by his or her desires, which are considered absolute.' (*AL*, 33)

Created for Relationship

Like any parent, I can look at my children and recognise them as individuals. They all have their own gifts, strengths and weaknesses. We have always encouraged our children to be themselves, not a copy of someone else. We want them to be seen as individuals – but that does not mean we are raising them to be individualistic. One of the constant challenges of family life is encouraging individual, strong personalities to live together as a family, to care about the needs and desires of others, to grow beyond their own ego. Our culture encourages the individual's personal autonomy and freedom of choice. Taken in a balanced way those can be positive forces. The difficulty comes when we lose sense of who we truly are, when we fail to see that we are created for relationship, that our greatest strength comes not from standing alone but standing together. When we focus on the unholy trinity of 'me, myself and I' we begin to define ourselves in terms of what we possess, what we achieve, what we earn. Our own advancement becomes the driving force in our lives and we lose the sense of responsibility to the community and particularly to those who are weakest or most isolated in the community.

The survival of the fittest is not a concept we find in the gospel but it exists in our society. That is why we need protection for family life, because it is a vulnerable and precious thing. We need good public policy on taxation and employment. We need affordable housing and protection for those who are struggling. Our Irish constitution talks about cherishing all the children of Ireland equally. We need this to be a reality in terms of access to education, healthcare and opportunities. Family life has enough challenges of its own without our social system creating more.

The spirituality of family life challenges rampant individualism and materialism. We are reminded that we are more than just our material bodies. We are a balance of body, mind and spirit and need to be nurtured at all those levels. That is not something we can do in isolation. If we take our Baptism seriously then we know we are baptised into a community of faith, into the body of Christ and that we are interdependent just as all the parts of the body depend on each other. So then my sense of self is that I am created in the image and likeness of God. I know myself in terms of who I am – not what I have or what I do – and I see myself as existing in relationship with God, with others and with the earth.

How does that impact on the relationships we build? Firstly, we are challenged to see all people as created in the image and likeness of God. Pope Francis has often talked about the dangers of a throwaway culture in which people are cast aside:

We treat affective relationships the way we treat material objects and the environment: everything is disposable; everyone uses and throws away, takes and breaks, exploits and squeezes to the last drop. Then, goodbye. (*AL*, 39)

That tendency to see people as valuable so long as they are useful, productive or bring pleasure impacts powerfully on our society. We see it in personal relationships, where people are cast aside on the basis that 'you don't make me happy any more'. However, we also see it shaping work practices and attitudes to people who struggle to find employment. People are defined in terms of their ability to earn and be productive. That really impacts on people who are older, suffer from ill-health or have special needs.

My gorgeous godson Eddie has Down syndrome. I have been reading a lot recently about government policies in countries such as Denmark and Iceland to be 'Downs free' within the next twenty years. Who gets to decide that a life with Down syndrome or any other disability is not a life worth living? It is true that Eddie may never contribute much in terms of taxes paid but is that a measure of his life? Like any of us Eddie has his moments when he is in a grump. He is no angel but if we are created for relationship then Eddie has that down to a fine art. It may sound like a cliché but Eddie really does bring out the best in people. If we are raising our children and challenging ourselves to treat everyone as being created in the image and likeness of God, then that applies to Eddie just as much as it does to his big brother Joseph.

The man who lives with mental illness or the woman who is crippled with arthritis, the elderly couple living in sheltered housing or the traveller family down the road – all are created in the image and likeness of God. That needs to be more than a pleasant idea. It needs to shape our public policy, our community building and our parish outreach.

If the pleasure principle is the driving force in our lives, then we are likely to live for the moment and the pleasure this moment can give us. Pope Francis talks about the 'culture of the ephemeral' (*AL*, 39) in which everything is seen as fleeting, short-lived and lacking permanence. Is it any wonder that a lifetime commitment seems too much, too challenging to be possible? If we are looking at marriage and family life from the perspective of the pleasure principle what do we see? There is the wonderful build up and excitement of the wedding but then what? Pleasure and delight? Yes, of course there is but that pleasure and delight are interwoven with challenges, frustrations, tensions and humdrum reality.

How could developing a spirituality of marriage and family life open us up to a different perspective? It begins with an awareness that we are part of a bigger story, part of a faith community and that our choice to commit to marriage and family life is supported by that faith community. So marriage is not just an event in the life of two people, or even their families but in the life of the whole community. We are tapping into the story of this community – past, present and future – the marriages that have built it, the families that have strengthened it and we are committing ourselves to be part of that story.

There is also a need to enter into marriage and family life with a realistic optimism. The pleasure principle dictates that we have an entitlement to pleasure and a right to avoid pain. Life in reality is more complex than that. Certainly in the Gospel Jesus said, 'I have come that you may have life and have it to the full' (Jn 10:10) but what he is offering is a richness of life, not guaranteed pleasure. If we nurture a spirituality of family life, then that will include an understanding that the paschal mystery is part of life. Pope Francis promotes marriage as 'a dynamic path to personal development and fulfilment' (*AL*, 37). To grow together in love, to become more truly and authentically ourselves, to expand our love to welcome children, these are the challenges we face. They will demand that we grow and develop in our maturity, our generosity and our capacity to support each other. We do not seek pain and suffering but a strong spirituality helps us recognise that life brings both blessing and challenge. Such a spirituality can build resilience and hope, giving us courage to withstand the storm.

If faith and life flow together then we are challenged to live with integrity. What we believe needs to shape our lives and the choices we make. Christian faith does not wrap us in cotton wool and protect us from the world. No, instead it sends us out into life, to see the world as God sees it, in all its wonder and with all its tragedy. How then could we stand by silently while families are made homeless, people enslaved, countries destroyed by war, fleeing families drowned at sea? None of us can change everything but we can each commit to changing something. We need to get actively involved and help our children to see that this is not how the world has to be.

What has all of this to do with the World Meeting of Families which will take place in Ireland in 2018? We are being offered an opportunity here to be creative, to offer families ways to engage with their faith, to grow together. I suggest that one of the most important things we could do is to commit to developing a strong spirituality of family life. Where do we begin? We need to create opportunities for people to talk about faith, to take ownership of their experience of God.

That may sound idealistic but bear with me a moment … I have seen it with my own eyes, people will talk about faith if they are given a chance and asked the right questions. For many years now I have worked with parents of children preparing for sacraments. I invite them, in small groups, to explore questions such as:

- Why do you want your child to have faith?
- What do you want your child to believe in?
- How do you want faith to shape your child's life?
- What echoes do you see between family life and what we celebrate at Mass?

They begin quietly, shy to talk about something as private as faith. Quickly however the energy and the sound level rise. Why? People begin to recognise and claim their own experience of God, in their own families. Telling someone God is at the heart of their life doesn't work nearly as well as enabling them to explore and find the presence and action of God themselves. At the moment we do not have enough of those opportunities.

The spirituality of family life has implications for how we prepare couples for marriage, how we raise our children, how we live as families and how we build our society. We are called to be a living gospel, bringing God's transforming love to bear in the world through the choices we make and the relationships we build.

Reflection Questions

1. Is there a phrase or image that remains with you from this chapter?

2. What could the spirituality of family life offer to you, your family and the wider community?

3. How do concepts such as holy ground, incarnation and paschal mystery speak to your experience of family life?

Endnote

1. Rolheiser, R. *The Holy Longing: The Search for a Christian Spirituality Image*; reissue edition 19 June 2009

Chapter Three
Looking to Jesus: the Vocation of the Family

FRANK AND ELIZABETH REYNOLDS

Looking to Jesus

The decision to call a Synod on the Family produced huge speculation that Pope Francis was going to change aspects of Church teaching in regard to marriage, family and sexuality. When Elizabeth and I were asked to pen our thoughts about chapter three of *Amoris Laetitia*, we had already gathered from the media that this had not happened. Marriage was still to be understood as a faithful, indissoluble union between a man and a woman, open to children as an expression of their love. This union was seen as a sacrament reflecting Christ's love for the Church. So, we wondered, what is the point of an exhortation which merely re-states church teaching?

Things did not get better when we saw that chapter three would 'summarise the Church's teaching on marriage and the family'. It is not that we disagree with the teaching at all. We accept the teaching role is central to what the Church does. In fact, as the Protestants emphasise the primacy of Scripture and the Orthodox Churches proclaim the beauty of right worship of God, the Catholic Church proclaims that its teaching is from God and that as a Church we should be united in adherence to the teaching of the magisterium. This does prompt two questions. How accessible is this teaching to the lay faithful? And how does this teaching relate to the day-to-day lives of married couples and families?

For the first question, it is best to begin with honesty. Perhaps like many lay Catholics, Elizabeth and I do not normally read the major Church documents; encyclicals and exhortations are not our bedtime reading. When the editor rang and asked us to write something about chapter three of *Amoris Laetitia*, we agreed (as one does without thinking) and then, when we put the phone down, I asked Elizabeth 'What is it called again?' By one of those odd coincidences, Elizabeth had bought a copy some months before, so we began a frantic search to find it (which took us two days). To be entirely fair, the writing of Pope Francis is more accessible than many Church documents, but how many will read it?

The second question regarding how this teaching relates to the day-to-day lives of families is important because if the teaching does not relate meaningfully to our daily lives, then what is its relevance? There may be a problem with teaching that is communicated in theologically dense documents which are not easy for the non-theologian to read. Such documents may be a perfect communication of correct teaching, but what does all this mean for you and me in the pew?

It is in the specific areas concerning marriage and decisions about having (or not having) children that the Church 'draws most critical fire' in the modern world. The decision about the use of contraceptives, outlined in *Humanae Vitae*, seemed to drive a wedge between the doctrinal teaching of the Church and the lives of ordinary Catholics. Add to this a perception that the teaching comes from an unmarried clerical elite who may know little about the ordinary lives of families, and the result is a sense of alienation between the laity and the Church hierarchy, and more important, between the laity and aspects of Church teaching. Many good Catholics are completely faithful to the teaching of their Church, but we can't deny that many people have moved to the margins of the Church and, while still being members, feel that some Church teaching needs to change to be relevant to their lives. That raises a further question: is the solution to be found in changing the teaching?

Some years ago before Mass, our priest asked me to find someone who would help bring up the offertory gifts. I approached an older man sitting near the back of the church and asked if he would help. He whispered quietly to me that he could not because 'I am a divorced man and shouldn't even be here'. He was attending Mass, sitting just inside the door and never coming forward for communion. He was quietly accepting that there was 'no way back' for him. He understood the doctrinal position of the Church and his perception was that he must, in a metaphorical sense, remain 'outside the walls'. His divorce from his wife had resulted in a second divorce from a Church of which he clearly still longed to be a part. This is dreadfully sad and even today as I think about that man, I cannot help but recall what Jesus said about the Pharisees: 'They find heavy burdens hard to bear, and lay them on men's shoulders; but they themselves will not move them with their finger.' (Mt: 23:4)

It can justifiably be argued that this man has a place in the Church and is welcome, although he cannot partake in Communion. However, his perception of not being welcome is shared quite widely and that is a problem for the Church. Encouragingly, we think that Pope Francis is seeking to address this in the exhortation.

A New Pentecost

Against this background we began to read *Amoris Laetitia*. Pope Francis begins with a statement which left us somewhat puzzled: 'In and among families, the Gospel message should always resound; the core of that message, the kerygma, is what is "most beautiful, most excellent, most appealing and at the same time most necessary".' (*AL,* 58)

We had to search the internet to find out that the kerygma is the initial proclamation of the Gospel and it is with this proclamation that Pope Francis introduces us to his summary of Church teaching on marriage and the family. The temptation on reading this document might be to skip the opening three paragraphs, but that would be a mistake. The kerygma is the proclamation of the message of the love and tenderness of God and if that is not at the heart of the Church's teaching, then Pope Francis writes that the teaching 'becomes nothing more than the defence of a dry and lifeless doctrine' (*AL,* 59). How many Catholics feel that some of the Church teachings on marriage, sexuality and family have been dry doctrines which lacked relevance to their lives? That many feel it is difficult to defend some aspects of Catholic teaching is what makes the opening paragraphs of *Amoris Laetitia* so important. Pope Francis is clearly placing his summary of Church teaching within the divine context of the Good News of the love of God. He is primarily preaching the Good News, the Gospel, and, more particularly, the 'Gospel of the family' (*AL,* 60).

Pope Francis gives this chapter the title 'Looking to Jesus: the Vocation of the Family'. Gazing at Our Lord he then goes on to invoke what Elizabeth and I felt was a stunning prayer for a new Pentecost for modern families: 'I now wish to turn my gaze to the living Christ, who is at the heart of so many love stories, and to invoke the fire of the Spirit upon all the world's families' (*AL,* 59).

This is the language of renewal. Before dealing with matters of doctrine or catechesis, we are directed to look to Jesus and the proclamation of the Good News. This has to be at the heart of our call as Christians. What we see is a Jesus who: 'Looked upon the women and men whom He met with love and tenderness, accompanying their steps in truth, patience and mercy as he proclaimed the demands of the Kingdom of God' (*AL*, 60).

Our sense is that these words are of key importance not only to this exhortation but to the papacy of Pope Francis. He is pointing us to a Jesus who does two things. First, he accompanies us on our human journey and, rather than leave people 'outside the walls' by condemning and judging them, he went to the cross outside the walls to save them. Second, Jesus teaches us the demands and the meaning of the Kingdom and how it relates to our lives and circumstances. It is not about changing the teaching, but about removing the condemnation and reaching out to couples and families 'where they are at'. When we meet the Lord where we are, no matter how far we fall short of the ideal, then with his grace we can begin to grow. Pope Francis is preaching a Gospel of Hope.

To look to Christ will include looking to Scripture and one of the strengths of this exhortation is that Pope Francis gathers together the main Biblical texts that concern marriage. In a section entitled 'Jesus Restores and Fulfils God's Plan', Pope Francis presents indissoluble marriage not as a yoke, but as a gift in which 'God's indulgent love always accompanies our human journey'. His love 'through grace ... heals and transforms hardened hearts, leading them back to the beginning through the way of the cross.' (*AL*, 62)

The hardness of heart mentioned here is from Jesus' teaching on marriage and divorce in Matthew 19:3-12. Jesus brings the discussion about divorce back to 'the beginning' when God 'made them male and female' and they were to be 'no longer two but one flesh'. The Pharisees question this teaching because Moses allowed divorce. Jesus' reply was that this was permitted 'for your hardness of heart' (Mt 19:8). In other words, the teaching was changed and no longer reflected God's plan in Genesis. As some in the Church demand that teaching must change to reflect our modern thinking, are we in danger of resisting the grace of God who seeks to heal and transform hardened hearts?

Jesus' mission, in all its aspects, was to restore 'God's original plan'. Marriage in this context takes its full meaning in Christ and his Church because 'Christ bestows on marriage and the family the grace necessary to bear witness to the love of God and to live the life of communion'. (*AL*, 63). In effect, Pope Francis is stating that marriage restored according to God's plan is an icon, an image of the Trinity. As married couples and families, our vocation is to witness by our daily lives the mystery of God's love for His people, of Our Lord's love for his spouse, the Church.

This is not new in Church teaching. Pope Benedict XVI, in the encyclical *Deus Caritas Est*, wrote: 'Marriage based on an exclusive and definitive love becomes an icon of the relationship between God and his people, and vice versa'. (*AL*, 70)

In our living room we have a reproduction of Andrei Rublev's icon of the Trinity, in which the Three Persons are seated round a table. When our children were younger and family meals around the table were the norm, Elizabeth and I used to think that there was something of a family likeness to this icon, that, in the 'ups and downs of family life', there was a faint reflection of God. It sounded (and sounds) fanciful, but this is what Pope Francis is saying. Scripture and tradition tell us of a 'Trinity which is revealed with the features of a family … the family is the image of God'. (*AL*, 71)

The Vocation of Marriage and Family

Vocation is a big word to Catholics. Traditionally we have understood a vocation as referring to those called by God to a celibate life in the priesthood or religious life. There was even an impression that the married state was something of a lower order of sanctity. Pope Francis is quite clear that marriage is a vocation:

> ... inasmuch as it is a response to a specific call to experience conjugal love as an imperfect sign of the love between Christ and the Church. Consequently, the decision to marry and to have a family ought to be the fruit of a process of vocational discernment. (*AL,* 72)

This marks a clear teaching that a married man and woman, who – with their bodies express their love for each other – are reflecting the image of God who embraced our humanity in the incarnation, and a Lord whose love for his bride, the Church is an eternal and indissoluble covenant.

Living this marriage covenant for us means 'every family, *despite its weaknesses,* can become a light in the darkness of our world' (*AL,* 66) and can 'bear witness to the Gospel of God's love' (*AL,* 71). This is a huge claim and it has implications for Catholic families and for how the Church prepares couples for marriage and family. The family exists not only for the sanctification of the couple and any children they are blessed with, but also for the Church, and even as a good for wider society. The exhortation quotes Pope Paul VI's *Address in Nazareth* where he says of the family: '... how fundamental and incomparable its role in the social order'. (*AL,* 66)

This teaching on marriage presents a high ideal. The danger is that it can appear to be aimed at spiritual elites. How can this understanding of marriage and family be translated meaningfully for ordinary Catholics? Who among priests, religious and catechists has the training necessary? And how do they engage with Catholic engaged couples, many of whom may regard attendance at a pre-marriage course as a chore, something required but not welcomed by them? Possibly the way ahead in this challenge is to build on the foundational work being done by lay organisations such as that of ACCORD in Ireland. To start this work with couples approaching marriage is already somewhat late. The 'gospel of the family' needs to begin in the home and in the school, it needs to be lived in loving families – it needs witnesses. It needs you and me.

And witness will be evident in our attitude to children who, from the moment of conception, are accepted as a fruit of a love which 'refuses every impulse to close in on itself' (*AL*, 80). Two things must be noted; the couple to whom God does not grant children are in no way diminished in their love; and the responsibility to plan a family still lies with the parents who are open to this gift. The family in God's plan is a sanctuary of life, from conception to the final stages of life. This is the vocation for those called to follow Our Lord in the married state.

The exhortation rightly indicates the challenge of raising children in the modern 'cultural reality' (*AL*, 84). With all the influences that bear on our youth in the age of the internet and social media, there has not been a more difficult time to raise a family. We ourselves have raised two sons in a period when the ubiquitous mobile phone means that whatever they are doing, they are continually connected to friends, the web and social media. To encourage them to give attention to matters of faith is a struggle and we feel that parents need help in this task.

Pope Francis clearly teaches that parents remain the primary educators of their children with schools complementing this role. Yet the exhortation points to a rift opening up 'between the family and society, between family and school' (*AL*, 84). The rights of the family as first educators of the children may be undermined by values in the curriculum in regard to marriage, sexuality, gender and procreation which are at variance to those held by Church members.

Recently, Elizabeth and I met a Lutheran pastor from Germany who asked us about schooling in Ireland, particularly in terms of what values are being taught to the children. He himself is a grandfather and told of a difficult choice his daughter and her husband had to face. In their region of Germany all nine-year old children are shown a sex-education video in class. The video does not deal with any values around relationships but basically and almost pornographically portrays sexual roles between a man and woman. This is part of the curriculum and opting to remove your child is not an option. The parents were deeply concerned about the matter and asked the pastor what they should do. His advice was to choose the lesser of two evils and go to the doctor and say that their son is sick and request a sick note.

The young couple wish themselves to introduce their children to teaching about relationships in a Christian context. Their concerns are so strong that they are considering home schooling as an alternative. In Ireland we are, thankfully, still some way from this level of a rift between family and school. We are fortunate in the excellent teaching in our Catholic schools and should be careful about safeguarding it. However, society is changing. That the Church, according to Pope Francis, is to cooperate with parents 'through suitable pastoral initiatives' may become even more important where an aggressively pluralistic society betrays its own values by refusing to tolerate the beliefs of the faith community.

Whatever the challenges presented by a secular society, few, if any, married couples can live up to the ideals of Catholic marriage. Helpfully the Holy Father picks up the theme of 'caring for those plants that are wilting and must not be neglected' (AL, 76).

What the exhortation calls 'imperfect situations' in relationships are not hard for us to find. We will recognise them perhaps even within our own families. Elizabeth and I have for some years been involved with ACCORD which delivers pre-marriage courses and counselling to couples or individuals for whom the problems in their relationship have become unmanageable. ACCORD is part of the Church's pastoral ministry and we do not judge or condemn people, but listen and share what we have for whatever time we have with them. From our experience in counselling couples, Elizabeth and I feel that these are mainly good people struggling with burdens they feel that they cannot bear. Pope Francis is calling on the Church family to show pastoral care to those who have fallen short of the ideal marriage or family. He is calling for the Church to reach out to those in civil marriages, the divorced and remarried. The Church has to find out how to make this practical, to make this a reality at parish level. That divorced man at the back of our Church during Mass must be given a sense that he belongs there.

Over recent years our diocese, Down and Connor, has initiated a 'Living Church' project. One of the pillars of this programme is that each parish should be 'a welcoming community'. The initial Living Church report, which was largely based on 'listening events' throughout the diocese, spoke with concern about those who feel excluded, specifically mentioning those in 'second relationships'. In *Amoris Laetitia* the Holy Father again looks to Jesus who in his encounters with people demonstrates 'the true meaning of mercy'. He does not condemn the woman found in adultery (cf. Jn 8:1-11), nor the Samaritan Woman at the well (who has had five husbands!) (cf. Jn 4:4-30). The centrality of mercy is clear in the conversations Jesus has with these two women. Pope Francis writes: '… the consciousness of sin is awakened by an encounter with Jesus' gratuitous love'. (*AL*, 64)

For many people who find themselves in 'imperfect situations' (in civil or second marriages, or living together) the encounter with their priest can be pivotal in how they will view the Church. Pope Francis call on priests to 'exercise careful discernment of situations'. Like Jesus they are to 'be attentive ... to how people experience and endure distress because of their condition' (*AL*, 79). Like Jesus, they are still to teach the Gospel, but in the context of mercy and loving care.

Elizabeth and I began with the question, 'What is the point of an exhortation which restates Church teaching?' For us the answer is that the teaching grows out of the love of God as revealed in Christ. The teaching on matters relating to marriage, family and children stem from God's plan in Genesis, are renewed in the redemptive work of Jesus and the guidance of the Holy Spirit in His Church. In recent decades the Church has been portrayed as standing, somewhat like King Canute, against the inevitable tide of 'progress'. Pope Francis is doing something very different. The context is not conservative versus liberal: the context is the proclamation of the Gospel of a loving God who came to be one of us, to share our broken humanity and bring hope.

In Luke 3:10, the people ask John the Baptist: 'What then shall we do?' We as Church need to ask the same question. One of the bravest things a young person can do today is to commit to marriage. Fear of commitment is very real and co-habitation is now very easy. For those already married, especially with so many spouses both working, life is busy. In the family world of making meals, doing homework, the school run and evening children's clubs, we need to find how to communicate this 'gospel of the family'.

Surely we have to follow Pope Francis and look to Jesus to know what we must do. As Jesus spread the Gospel by being among people in their ordinary lives, so should the message of *Amoris Laetitia* be brought down to parish level, where it can be accessible to all of us. Ireland has an amazing opportunity in that the World Meeting of Families in 2018 is to take place in Dublin, hopefully with Pope Francis present. The Pope's prayer for renewal, quoted above, should be our shared prayer. 'I now wish to turn my gaze to the living Christ, who is at the heart of so many love stories, and to invoke the fire of the Spirit upon all the world's families'. (*AL,* 59)

There is a remarkable statement in the exhortation which summarises the complete theme of the Pope's thought in the exhortation: 'Within the family "which could be called a domestic church" (*Lumen Gentium*, 11), individuals enter upon an ecclesial experience of communion among persons, which reflects, through grace, the mystery of the Holy Trinity'. (*AL,* 86)

Our attitudes to work, caring for others, forgiveness, prayer and our understanding of our role in life begin in the family. How many saints witness to the influence of their parents and their family, often very humble families? The safeguarding of marriage is a concern to a Church which is itself a 'family of families', a living organism in which the family and the church exist for each other, strengthening and building up the Kingdom of God. In the family, through all its joys and challenges, the love of God is to be alive to all family members in a way which is essential for the Church and to our wider society. Do we want renewal in the Church? Let us begin with renewal in marriage and the family.

Reflection Questions

1. Do you think that *Amoris Laetitia* is simply re-stating Church teaching on marriage and the family? Or is it doing something else?

2. What are the biggest obstacles families face in living out their Christian mission?

3. Look at *Amoris Laetitia*, 61. Which of the quotations from Scripture speak to you in particular?

4. How can we begin with renewal in marriage and the family?

Chapter Four

Love in Marriage

BREDA O'BRIEN

In Thornton Wilder's beautiful play, *Our Town*, one of the characters, Emily Webb, has died but is allowed to return briefly from death to be invisibly present at her own twelfth birthday. At this celebration, she desperately tries to make her mother see her twelve-year-old self, really see her, but fails because her mother is busy doing all the things that mothers do. She begs her, 'Oh Mama, please look at me one minute as though you really saw me?' She breaks down and asks to go back to her grave, but before she goes, she bursts out, 'Do any human beings realise life as they live it? Every, every minute?'

In this play, the stage manager is a character. He is present on stage and tells her that human beings rarely realise the immensity and importance of life as they live it, 'except saints and poets, maybe'. *Amoris Laetitia* can be read as an attempt by Pope Francis to get us to see, really see, our families and their significance in God's plan. He talks about the everyday pain caused by not feeling seen, which 'lies behind the complaints and grievances we often hear in families: "My husband does not look at me; he acts as if I were invisible". "Please look at me when I am talking to you!"' (*AL,* 128)

Elsewhere, he quotes complaints made in families, words that probably echo worries he has heard many times in a long life as a pastor. For example, he says 'how often we hear complaints like: "He does not listen to me." "Even when you seem to, you are really doing something else."' (*AL,* 137) He is fully aware of the human need to be seen and acknowledged and also that many families fail each other in big and small ways. These insights into ordinary family hurts give the document a level of realism, which make the Pope's vision of the family also seem more credible. He sees the love found in families as sharing in the divine character, even though family life is also a place of ordinary frailty. This is the message that will be reiterated in many ways in preparation for and celebration of the World Meeting of Families in Ireland in 2018.

I Corinthians 13: 4-7

In order to help us to see the centrality of the family in God's plan more clearly, in chapter four, 'Love in Marriage' he focuses on an exegesis of I Corinthians 13: 4-7, and in chapter five, 'Love Made fruitful' he examines how love always leads to life, whether that life be literal children or other ways of being fruitful.

> Love is patient, love is kind;
> Love is not jealous or boastful; it is not arrogant or rude.
> Love does not insist on its own way, it is not irritable or resentful;
> It does not rejoice at wrong, but rejoices in the right.
> Love bears all things, believes all things, hopes all things, endures all things. (1 Cor 13:4-7)

His choice of 1 Corinthians 13 is both appealing and unexpected. While virtually every Catholic is familiar with the passage (it is used so often, particularly at weddings) we may have grown numb to its message or even dismiss it as hackneyed. Yet, as Pope Francis points out, 'all that has been said so far would be insufficient to express the Gospel of marriage and the family, were we not also to speak of love' (*AL,* 89) and Paul's treatment of love is unrivalled in Scripture. In the same way as he wishes us to see the vocation that all families share more clearly, perhaps the Pope wishes us to see this well-known passage with clearer eyes, too, especially because of its emphasis on love as acts, not feelings. Quoting the *Catechism of the Catholic Church*, he cautions that the word love 'is commonly used and often misused.' (*AL*, 89) This is true both for those who are secular and those who are Christian, because Christians are as immersed in culture as anyone else is. In our times, a particular vision of romantic love has taken precedence, one that prioritises personal fulfilment and the happiness of the individuals concerned. Pope Francis does not criticise this view directly. Instead, he spends chapter four describing how love manifests itself in attitudes and actions, which implicitly suggests that a vision of love that is primarily based on feelings and personal fulfilment falls far short of what is possible. However, while presenting an ideal the Pope does not impose an impossible burden of always living up to that ideal, because tenderness, forgiveness and mercy are always presented as essential expressions of real love, too.

Many, including the Vatican authors of the summary of *Amoris Laetitia*, have noted how psychological and theological insights have been integrated very well by Pope Francis.

> The quality of psychological introspection that marks
> this exegesis is striking. The psychological insights enter
> into the emotional world of the spouses – positive
> and negative – and the erotic dimension of love. This
> is an extremely rich and valuable contribution to
> Christian married life, unprecedented in previous papal
> documents.[1]

There is ample evidence of psychological insights gained from a lifetime of patient listening to members of families as a pastor. However, the ultimate goal is not just to create more psychologically healthy families, but families that bring Christ to the world. A distinction made by Dr Gerald May, a psychiatrist who devoted much of his life to spirituality, may be useful here. He often said that the goal of psychotherapy was to make the client more comfortable, but that this sometimes came into conflict with the spiritual needs of the person, because discomfort could bring that person closer to surrendering to God. His obituarist in the *Washington Post* sums it up like this: 'There's a difference of intent,' [May] once told a reporter. 'Therapy deals with relationships, feelings and the goal of leading more efficient lives. Spiritual direction deals with prayer life and one's experience of God.'[2]

While there are many insights, including psychological insights, in Pope Francis' writings, they are all subordinate to a higher goal – of reaching union with God and making real his love in the world. Yet it is striking how the insights of psychologists and researchers often mirror insights expressed by Paul in the First century. For example, Dr John Gottman is a renowned clinical psychologist and researcher who has shown that four factors predict whether couples will divorce or not, and they all have to do with styles of communication. Dr Gottman nicknamed them the 'Four Horsemen of the Apocalypse', a metaphor based on Revelations 6, where the horsemen are agents of destruction which arrive before the Last Judgement and symbolise conquest, war, hunger, and death respectively. In relationships, the Four Horsemen that signal a kind of apocalypse in a relationship are criticism, contempt, defensiveness and stonewalling. Criticism that damages to this degree is of a particular kind: attacking the person, rather than specific actions of the person. (To be clear, when Gottman says criticism is destructive, he does not believe that people should passively accept damaging actions by others, but that the focus should always be on the impact of the actions, not the essence of the person.) Similarly, contempt is corrosive. According to Dr Gottman, expressing contempt for a spouse, especially to others, is the single biggest predictor of divorce. Defensiveness prevents dialogue, because it implicitly blames the other person for the division in the relationship. Until people can begin to acknowledge their own part in the breakdown of a relationship without being defensive, healing is impossible. Stonewalling is the fourth factor identified by Gottman and other researchers, and occurs when someone cuts him or herself off from all interaction and becomes impossible to reach. The insights of Paul's letters are protective against all four horsemen, and can build relationships that have a greater chance of surviving in a way that protects both partners and any children they may have. But this is not the end-game. All our relationships can also bring us closer to, or further away from God.

Love as Acts, not Feelings

For example, when Pope Francis explores the characteristics of love, starting with *makrothyméi*, translated as patience, he is doing so not just as someone with deep psychological insights. He sees patience as mirroring the kind of profound acceptance which God has for us. Acceptance is the opposite of criticising the essence of a person. Pope Francis says that, 'Love always has an aspect of deep compassion that leads to accepting the other person as part of this world, even when he or she acts differently than I would like.' (*AL,* 92) This kind of patience is notably absent from our culture. The Pope's insistence on patience also reminds me of Dr David Elkind's classic work, *The Hurried Child*, already more than thirty-five years old, but appearing more and more prescient with every year that passes. The developmental needs of children and adolescents are being ignored as childhood grows shorter and shorter. Young people are being pressured into precocious maturity, in part because their parents live in what Elkind described as 'a pressure cooker of competing demands, transitions, role changes, personal and professional uncertainties, over which he or she exerts slight direction.'[3] In compensation, adults have embraced the idea of the resilient child. Children are indeed resilient, but sometimes the concept is abused to the extent of even promoting as a good something which is stressful for children, such as being left at home alone at early ages. It induces too much guilt in parents to consider that children are suffering because of the changes forced upon them by adult decisions. The Pope, however, does not just have children in mind. He refers also to our impatience with significant people in our lives, our demand that they meet our expectations. 'We encounter problems whenever we think that relationships or people ought to be perfect, or when we put ourselves at the centre and expect things to turn out our way.' (*AL*, 92).

This is not just a matter of individual actions, but of habits that build us into being a particular kind of person. Pope Francis examines how Saint Paul uses the word *chrestéuetai*, derived from *chrestós*, meaning 'a good person, one who shows his goodness by his deeds' (*AL*, 93). Anyone familiar with Francis' works will know that the concepts of mercy, tenderness and kindness run like a golden thread through them. He uses the words 'mercy' and 'merciful' nearly forty times in this exhortation alone. However, in this instance, he is looking at the habit of being kind, or a person whose character is kind, in order to emphasise that patience is not just passive. The Pope concurs, it appears, with Henry James' aphorism: 'Three things in human life are

V. Imp

important: The first is to be kind. The second is to be kind. And the third is to be kind.'[4]

Sometimes the qualities that Saint Paul emphasises can seem in direct contrast to attitudes that are valued in our current culture. We live in a society driven by demand for more and more consumer goods, regardless of the impact on our environment. We are constantly encouraged to be dissatisfied both with ourselves and with what we have, a modern version of the sin of covetousness but one on which our economies depend. *Zelói*, meaning jealousy or envy, is used by Paul as an illustration of one of the characteristics which destroys love. The Pope links this to the covetousness proscribed in two of the commandments. Overcoming envy is not enough: we also have 'to find ways of helping society's outcasts to find a modicum of joy. That is not envy, but the desire for equality.' In other words, the antidote to covetousness is to share what we have with those who are most in need. In a similar way, a certain kind of arrogance is often rewarded in our society. Paul uses the terms *perpereúetai* and *physioútai*, both forms of arrogance or of being 'puffed up'. However, the Pope focuses on being 'puffed up' not because of what we possess but because we think we know better than others. He then applies these terms to those who are arrogant towards 'family members who are less knowledgeable about the faith, weak or less sure in their convictions' (*AL*, 98). Later on, in chapter eight, he emphasises that 'the Church's pastors, in proposing to the faithful the full ideal of the Gospel and the Church's teaching, must also help them to treat the weak with compassion, avoiding aggravation or unduly harsh or hasty judgements'. There is a clear echo here of the parable of the Pharisee and the tax collector – those who presume to know better than others, are in danger of falling into the sin of pride. Humility is a virtue that is essential in real love. There is an echo of this in chapter eight, when the Pope counsels that anyone entering into discernment about an 'irregular union' must do so under the following conditions: 'humility, discretion and love for the Church and her teaching, in a sincere search for God's will and a desire to make a more perfect response to it'. (*AL*, 300) Humility, therefore, is essential for everyone, including both those who see themselves as being in the right and those who acknowledge sinfulness. In a homily in November 2016, the Pope reiterated that humility is not something theatrical that draws attention to how humble we are. Instead, 'the humility of the childlike is that of somebody who walks in the presence of the Lord, does not speak badly about others, looks only at serving and feels that he or she is the smallest … That is where their strength lies.'5

Paul's term *aschemonéi*, often translated as rude, is also destructive of real love. To illustrate the virtue of courtesy, which is the antithesis of rudeness, the Pope quotes from what may be one of the most unusual sources ever cited in a papal document – a treatise on love and eroticism by Mexican poet and former diplomat, Octavio Paz. He cites Paz's definition of courtesy. It 'is a school of sensitivity and disinterestedness' which requires a person 'to develop his or her mind and feelings, learning how to listen, to speak and, at certain times, to keep quiet' (*AL*, 99).6 The Pope is referencing here what used to be described as 'custody of the tongue' in Benedictine spirituality. Again, this is a theme that recurs in Francis' writing and homilies. He emphasises again and again the importance of kindness in our words:

> Words can build bridges between individuals and
> within families, social groups and peoples. This is
> possible both in the material world and the digital

world. Our words and actions should be such as to help us all escape the vicious circles of condemnation and vengeance which continue to ensnare individuals and nations, encouraging expressions of hatred. The words of Christians ought to be a constant encouragement to communion and, even in those cases where they must firmly condemn evil, they should never try to rupture relationships and communication.[7]

Criticism which attacks the person, or contempt which condemns, always weaken relationships. However, when he carries out an exegesis of a phrase like *ou logízetai to kakón*, which means that love takes no account of evil, he is not talking just about psychological mechanisms in a couple's relationship, as a relationship expert like John Gottman might, but about the movement of grace in our lives.

> If we accept that God's love is unconditional, that the Father's love cannot be bought or sold, then we will become capable of showing boundless love and forgiving others even if they have wronged us. Otherwise, our family life will no longer be a place of understanding, support and encouragement, but rather one of constant tension and mutual criticism. (*AL,* 108)

Forgiveness is also essential to love, not just once, but again and again. In a long passage from Martin Luther King, the Pope explores the kind of love that exhibits 'a certain dogged heroism, a power to resist every negative current, an irrepressible commitment to goodness' (*AL,* 118). He particularly praises those who, despite infidelity and other hurts, continue to love someone from whom they have been forced to separate for their own protection, by trying to help the other partner when they are ill or undergoing suffering and other trials. 'Love does not yield to resentment, scorn for others or the desire to hurt or to gain some advantage. The Christian ideal, especially in families, is a love that never gives up.' In proposing this kind of love, Pope Francis is proposing a love that makes itself known in both attitudes and concrete actions. It is not in any way airy-fairy. It can be measured by its fruits.

On a personal note, I feel that the Pope's vision of love is a much-needed corrective to the culture of 'the one', that is, the idea that there is someone out there who is 'the one' for you, who will fulfil all your needs. It is an impossible burden for any one person or any one relationship to carry. Instead, by focusing on the traits that lead to successful relationships, such as patience, kindness, forgiveness and endurance, the Pope is pointing to a different model of relationship, where the kind of person that you are and the willingness to bring love to every situation is more important than some kind of static ideal mate who inspires devotion because they meet your needs so perfectly. 'This joy, the fruit of fraternal love, is not that of the vain and self-centred, but of lovers who delight in the good of those whom they love, who give freely to them and thus bear good fruit.' (*AL,* 129) This love can be made concrete in the simplest of ways, including the Pope's often expressed advice that marriage and family life can be immeasurably enriched by the use of 'three words: "Please", "Thank you", "Sorry". Three essential words!' (*AL,* 133). The papal exhortation never loses this homely quality, this dedication to the simple things that we must do every day in order to have a happy family life.

The Nature of Conjugal Love

After his discussion of the passage from St Paul's Letter to the Corinthians, Pope Francis moves on to the nature of conjugal love, repeating Aquinas' insight that 'after the love that unites us to God, conjugal love is the 'greatest form of friendship … It is a union possessing all the traits of a good friendship: concern for the good of the other, reciprocity, intimacy, warmth, stability and the resemblance born of a shared life. Marriage joins to all this an indissoluble exclusivity expressed in the stable commitment to share and shape together the whole of life' (*AL*, 123). The Exhortation firmly and unequivocally re-states the importance of an indissoluble permanent commitment in marriage. Such a union is not easy, particularly in what Pope Francis dubs 'the culture of the ephemeral that prevents a constant process of growth.' (*AL*, 124) In an acknowledgement of the difficulties of life-long marriage, the Pope is careful to distinguish between joy, and mere happiness. Quoting Thomas Aquinas, he states that 'marriage is an inevitable mixture of enjoyment and struggles, tensions and repose, pain and relief, satisfactions and longings, annoyances and pleasures, but always on the path of friendship, which inspires married couples to care for one another' (*AL*, 126).

Perhaps this is one of the greatest contributions that the ideal of Christian marriage can bring to contemporary culture, which is indeed often a 'culture of the ephemeral'. There is ample research which shows that happily married couples have exactly the same amount of 'irreconcilable differences' as couples who break up.[8] The key difference is the way in which such differences are negotiated.

The document also explores the role of passion and eros in a marital relationship, and endorses their importance. Marriage is not all about self-sacrifice, because 'we need to remember that authentic love also needs to be able to receive the other, to accept one's own vulnerability and needs, and to welcome with sincere and joyful gratitude the physical expressions of love found in a caress, an embrace, a kiss and sexual union.' (*AL*, 157) This is as robust an endorsement of the joy of a couple's physical relationship as can be found. However, the Pope is also acutely aware that because sexuality is at the core of a person's identity, it can also be fraught and very prone to manipulation or, in extreme cases, even violence. The same realism that marks other passages of this document is found here, too.

Nor is the ideal of marriage presented in a way that makes those who remain virgins, or enter consecrated life or receive Holy Orders feel as though they have chosen a lesser path. 'Virginity and marriage are, and must be, different ways of loving.' (*AL*, 161) Just as he cautions about the distortions that can enter into married life, he also cautions against a kind of celibacy that is little more than a comfortable bachelorhood.

> Celibacy can risk becoming a comfortable single life
> that provides the freedom to be independent, to move
> from one residence, work or option to another, to spend
> money as one sees fit and to spend time with others as
> one wants. In such cases, the witness of married people
> becomes especially eloquent. (*AL*, 162)

In Pre-Vatican II times, a celibate vocation was seen (implicitly at least) as infinitely superior. Now we have moved to an understanding of the vocations of priesthood, religious life, the celibate single life and marriage as all being valid and valuable ways of loving. They all have the potential, in their challenges and joys, to bring us closer to the heart of God.

Reflection Questions

1. What words from I Corinthians 13 came to life for you while reading this chapter?

2. Do you think the current cultural model of romance, which focuses almost exclusively on the couple, is a sustainable one? What does *Amoris Laetitia* have to offer?

3. What do a mother and father bring to a family because they are male and female?

Endnotes

1. Summary of the post-Synodal Apostolic Exhortation *Amoris Laetitia* (The Joy of Love) on love in the family, 08.04.2016 https://press.vatican.va/content/salastampa/en/bollettino/pubblico/2016/04/08/160408b.html Accessed 1 Dec 2016

2. http://www.washingtonpost.com/wp-dyn/articles/A48245-2005Apr12.html

3. Elkind, D., *The Hurried Child*, Perseus Publishing; third edition (April 2001), p. 3

4. http://www.smithsonianmag.com/arts-culture/choosing-civility-in-a-rude-culture-97997109/#G6ddhOWgJ3FOXXv3.99 This quote comes from Leon, E., *Henry James: A Life, vol V: The Master 1901-1916*, Avon Books, 1972

5. http://en.radiovaticana.va/news/2016/11/29/pope_christian_humility_is_the_virtue_of_%E2%80%9Cthe_childlike%E2%80%9D_/1275580 Accessed December 1st, 2016

6. Paz, O. *The Double Flame – Essays on Love and Eroticism*, Kindle Edition, Location 432

7. Message of His Holiness Pope Francis for the 50th World Communications Day, http://w2.vatican.va/content/francesco/en/messages/communications/documents/papa-francesco_20160124_messaggio-comunicazioni-sociali.html Accessed 1 Dec 2016

8. https://www.gottman.com/blog/managing-conflict-solvable-vs-perpetual-problems/

Chapter Five
Love Made Fruitful
BREDA O'BRIEN

Love Always Brings Life

'Love always gives life' are the first words of this chapter. (*AL*, 165). The reader could almost stop here, because it summarises the rest of the chapter. Love, by its essence, is always life-giving. There is a strong focus on the obvious sense in which this statement is true. We are made male and female, and as a result of the attraction and love between a man and a woman, the next generation is given life. However, as Pope Francis makes clear, we are called to bring life in every aspect of our lives. It is an interesting test of all our interactions – do they bring life to others, or do they suck the life out of them? It reinforces a point made many times by the Pope. Our words and our interactions with others, no matter how simple they are, have consequences. Do they tend to bring life or the opposite?

We Love our Children because They are Children

Almost immediately, Pope Francis focuses on those who would deny the value of life. He says that the freely given love of God is reflected in the reality that 'children are loved even before they arrive.' But then he denounces those who say that some children should never have been born.

> From the first moments of their lives, many children are rejected, abandoned, and robbed of their childhood and future. There are those who dare to say, as if to justify themselves, that it was a mistake to bring these children

into the world. This is shameful! … How can we issue solemn declarations on human rights and the rights of children, if we then punish children for the errors of adults? (*AL,* 166)

This is clearly directed at those who use slogans such as 'every childish a wanted child' in order to deny children the right to life, or those who look at the economic costs of children as if that determined their right to be born or to access treatment. Although the Pope does not use this example, non-invasive pre-natal screening (NIPS) when used to identify and destroy the unborn, fits into this definition of a culture where children bear the brunt of adult decisions. In many ways, NIPS is a scientific breakthrough, because it replaces invasive pre-natal screening, which not only was less accurate but held a risk of miscarriage. In a culture that valued all human life, this technology would simply help parents prepare to greet, love and support the child who is to be born. However, it is being used instead by some to identify and eradicate children who have Down syndrome. The test is very expensive, but Patrick Willems, a paediatrician and CEO of a Belgian laboratory, Gendia, that offers the Harmony NIPS test for Down syndrome for sale on the internet has justified it. 'Preventing the birth of fifty babies with Down syndrome will offset the costs of fully implementing the NIPS into Dutch public healthcare,' he said. That led to a headline in a Dutch newspaper: 'A child with Down syndrome costs 1 to 2 million Euros.'[1] Are children to become subject to budget sheet calculations, and if they are too expensive, are they no longer to have a right to life? The Pope strongly rejects this kind of calculation. 'No sacrifice made by adults will be considered too costly or too great, if it means the child never has to feel that he or she is a mistake, or worthless or abandoned to the four winds and the arrogance of man.' (*AL,* 166)

Sally Phillips is a British actor and comedian, best known for her role in the *Bridget Jones' Diary* franchise. She has a son Ollie who has Down syndrome, and she is profoundly disturbed by the implications of NIPS. Since it has been implemented in Iceland, one hundred per cent of those whose babies were diagnosed with Down syndrome have been aborted. She interviewed people in Britain about NIPS. Phillips then travelled to Iceland to meet a young woman who speaks two languages, has a job and a boyfriend, and also Down syndrome, who protests against the eradication of people like her. Phillip's title for her documentary is the provocative question: *A World without Down Syndrome?* Sally Phillips is herself pro-choice, but her questions in the programme suggest that choice may have significant downsides. She herself never addresses the implications of querying choice as the ultimate value, but on viewing the programme (currently available on YouTube) a clear question emerges. If it is wrong to abort people because they have a mental handicap, why is it justifiable to abort anyone? As the Pope says, 'So it matters little whether this new life is convenient for you, whether it has features that please you, or whether it fits into your plans and aspirations. For 'children are a gift. Each one is unique and irreplaceable ... We love our children because they are children, not because they are beautiful, or look or think as we do, or embody our dreams. We love them because they are children. A child is a child.' (*AL*, 170) This is a powerful reiteration of the value of all life from conception to natural death.

Gender

Chapter five also looks at another contentious issue by examining the role of gender from many angles, starting with the pronouncement that: 'Every child has a right to receive love from a mother and a father; both are necessary for a child's integral and harmonious development …' (*AL*, 172). This statement would once have been seen as almost banal, but it is now questioned from many angles. Most recently, the idea that children need the love of both a mother and a father was considered insufficient reason to retain marriage as the union of a man and a woman both in the United States and Ireland. Same-sex marriage advocates proclaimed that marriage has nothing to do with children, thereby undermining both the idea that marriage is a gendered institution and that marriage, more often than not, leads to children. The Pope speaks against 'an ideology of gender' that 'denies the difference and reciprocity in nature of a man and a woman and envisages a society without sexual differences, thereby eliminating the anthropological basis of the family' (*AL*, 56).

In the worldview generated by this ideology of gender, parents are allegedly interchangeable and there is no particular benefit to having one of each gender. The Pope reinforces the idea that the genders are different, but does not reinforce the kind of rigid gender stereotypes most often associated with the 1950s. However, he reiterates that 'biological sex and the socio-cultural role of sex (gender) can be distinguished but not separated' (*AL*, 56). Rigid gender stereotyping is not good, but neither is the idea that biology has nothing to do with gender.

There are other cultural trends that have affected how we view gender roles. Feminism has made tremendous strides for women; the Pope endorses this progress, but with one caveat. 'Nowadays we acknowledge as legitimate and indeed desirable that women wish to study, work, develop their skills and have personal goals. At the same time, we cannot ignore the need that children have for a mother's presence, especially in the first months of life' (*AL*, 173). The most difficult questions are where there are clashes of legitimate rights. Women have the right to achieve their potential, but human babies are uniquely vulnerable. A kitten is born blind and completely helpless but within months is virtually independent. Humans remain utterly vulnerable for years. In my view, this problem is not easy to solve at an individual level. Women's worth does not stem solely from their ability to reproduce, but that does not make the ability less miraculous. However, our society downgrades this role, focusing again on economic criteria as if economic independence and contribution to the paid workforce were the markers of a valid human existence. Caring work is automatically downgraded in this worldview, as shown by the low wages paid to those who step in to replace the caring work of mothers and fathers – childcare workers. Until the culture as a whole stops viewing the male – unencumbered by caring duties – as the human ideal, and acknowledges that women play a unique role in the reproduction of the species, there will be little chance of overcoming the bias in favour of paid work. The Pope also reinforces the importance of fathers. 'God sets the father in the family so that by the gifts of his masculinity he can be "close to his wife and share everything, joy and sorrow, hope and hardship"' (*AL*, 177). Again, this is not a rigid gender role, but neither is it identical to women's roles. Being male and female is part of God's plan.

Going Beyond the Nuclear Family

The Catholic Church is often accused of being obsessed with the physical aspects of marriage and of setting physical reproduction as the highest goal of marriage. This is far from the case, which the Pope makes clear by repeating the words of one of the Vatican Documents: At the same time, we know that 'marriage was not instituted solely for the procreation of children … Even in cases where, despite the intense desire of the spouses, there are no children, marriage still retains its character of being a whole manner and communion of life, and preserves its value and indissolubility'.[2] So too, 'motherhood is not a solely biological reality, but is expressed in diverse ways'. (*AL,* 178)

These are important words, and tie in with the idea of fruitfulness being more than physical fruitfulness. It leads to an endorsement of adoption and fostering that is carried out in the best interests of the child, but also to one of the most challenging aspects of *Amoris Laetitia,* that real, authentic familial love cannot be confined to family and friends, but must go beyond it if it is to reach its full potential. The Pope emphasises that 'families should not see themselves as a refuge from society, but instead go forth from their homes in a spirit of solidarity with others …' and also that 'we must not forget that 'the "mysticism" of the sacrament [of the Eucharist] has a social character'. When those who receive it turn a blind eye to the poor and suffering, or consent to various forms of division, contempt and inequality, the Eucharist is received unworthily' (*AL,* 186). I presume I am not alone in suppressing an inward groan when I read these words in the papal exhortation. To be honest, building a strong culture of family life is so difficult that to be told bluntly that it is not enough even if you succeed is very challenging. It reminded me of a story someone once told me about Gustavo Gutiérrez, the liberation theologian. Apparently, after a talk he was asked what steps we should take to relieve poverty. His response surprised everyone, as it was expected that he would talk in terms of changing oppressive structures. Instead, he said that everyone should ensure that they have a relationship with a poor person in their lives. So he did not suggest taking to the streets to protest, or changing the way that society operates as the most important. He suggested that a personal relationship with someone would keep the needs of the poor to the forefront of our minds, and that other changes would flow from that motivation. This is immensely challenging, because it means that outreach to others is a central part of living an authentic Catholic family life, and so many parents find that they are barely managing all the other parts, like regular family and prayer time, not to mention constant catechesis of, listening to and conversation with those who are closest to them. It is not enough, even, to be actively involved in your Church community, hard as that may be in itself. There is an echo in Pope Francis' words of what Fr Michael Corcoran and Tom White wrote in their book, *Rebuilt*, which looks at how parish life may be renewed. They say the constant temptation is to build 'Churchworld', a space that is very comfortable for 'Churchpeople' and irrelevant to everyone else. But this only leads to stasis and decay. The Gospel demands a constant going out to others with the Good News.

Aside from challenging families to go outside themselves, Pope Francis also implicitly dismisses the nuclear family model, if it only consists of parents and children. He prefers an intergenerational model, saying that 'we must reawaken the collective sense of gratitude, of appreciation, of hospitality, which makes the elderly feel like a living part of the community'. Grandparents, grand-aunts and grand-uncles have a vital role to play in families. As a culture, we have moved away from the idea that we should consult people who are older and wiser, to a presumption that each generation knows more than the previous one, and that people who are two generations older have little to teach us. But nothing can replace life experience, because it often brings wisdom of a kind that is impossible to Google. 'A family that fails to respect and cherish its grandparents, who are its living memory, is already in decline, whereas a family that remembers has a future … Our contemporary experience of being orphans as a result of cultural discontinuity, up-rootedness and the collapse of the certainties that shape our lives, challenges us to make our families places where children can sink roots in the rich soil of a collective history.' (*AL*, 193)

In short, in chapter five, the Pope is urging us to build a model of family that is firmly founded on the love of a mother and father, but:

> this larger family should provide love and support
> to teenage mothers, children without parents, single
> mothers left to raise children, persons with disabilities
> needing particular affection and closeness, young people
> struggling with addiction, the unmarried, separated
> or widowed who are alone, and the elderly and infirm
> who lack the support of their children. It should also
> embrace 'even those who have made shipwreck of their
> lives'. (*AL*, 197)

The latter is a wonderful phrase: 'those who have made shipwreck of their lives.'[3] In his book, *What's So Amazing About Grace?*,[4] Philip Yancey describes a young woman who has really made a shipwreck of her life, falling into addiction and then prostitution in order to maintain the habit, leaving her child neglected. Someone urges her to seek help from a church, and she asks why she should do that, given that she already feels bad enough about herself? Yancey states that a Church which is seen only as a place that condemns rather than helps explains why so many people see faith as irrelevant to their lives. In chapters four and five of *Amoris Laetitia*, described as central to the document by the Pope, that same message echoes again and again. Real love is shown by our acts and habits, not by how we feel. Love is always fruitful. It brings life, not condemnation. It seeks to build a better world by coming closer to Christ and his vision for humanity. It is always full of tenderness and mercy. And that is the vision of Christian family life to which Pope Francis is calling us.

Reflection Questions

1. How can the parish support people whose lives are not lived according to the ideal of Christian marriage, but who sincerely wish to live Christian lives?

2. How far have gender roles evolved during your life?

3. What kind of outreach beyond the borders of your home might be possible in your family?

Endnotes

1. https://www.nrc.nl/nieuws/2015/10/06/en-kind-met-down-kost-1-tot-2-miljoen-euro-1542020-a250826

2. Second Vatican Ecumenical Council, Pastoral Constitution on the Church in the Modern World, *Gaudium et Spes*, 50

3. Catechesis (7 October 2015): *L'Osservatore Romano*, 8 October 2015, p. 8

4. Yancey, P. *What's so Amazing About Grace?*, Zondervan Publishing, 1997, p. 11

Chapter Six
Some Pastoral Perspectives

FRANKIE MURRAY

Pope Francis uses a beautiful phrase. He talks about the 'Gospel of the family'. The Gospel is Jesus: He came to bring the Good News of healing, compassion and forgiveness. Jesus embodied these words: He is the Word made Flesh. The family is a sacred place where these words of Jesus can find a home. The family can be, and often is a place of healing, forgiveness, security and unconditional love, the Home of Jesus where the Word is made flesh. Sadly, sometimes it can also cause deep wounds that can maim the rest of our lives.

Of course, every family needs a home, a place to live, to give the 'Gospel Word' a home. The exhortation is unambiguous in its call to denounce political or economic decisions that lead to exclusion and discrimination. The Irish families who have no home, the refugee camps of desperate people without a home or a homeland, are the cries in the wilderness seeking compassionate and generous hospitality, a place to call home.

The responses of families before the Synod on the Family stated that ordained ministers often lacked the skills and competence to deal with complex family problems. As priests, we need to listen to the experience of families. We need to learn from that experience. Families have much to teach. We have much to learn. We need the help of those qualified to help us and to be able to refer families to them for competent care.

The care and wisdom of the extended family and neighbours creates an environment of support in every community. The social worker, the doctor, the public health nurse, the teacher, the Gardaí, all have their part to play in the care of the family in distress. It is important that the training of seminarians be grounded in and guided by the reality, beauty and complexity of family life today. Pope Francis writes caringly about the preparation of couples for marriage, making the point that the best preparation for a couple is the example of their parents and their own home. The years of love, kindness and self-sacrifice that children learn from their parents is the greatest example and the most powerful influence. It never ceases to amaze me to see the energy and the effort, the care, time and expense that parents give to their children today. This love that does not 'count the cost' must surely bear fruit in the future to help tomorrow's adults discover the 'Joy of Love'. Here we must acknowledge the gift that is ACCORD. For over sixty years this outstanding group of lay volunteers and priests has offered marriage support, counselling and preparation for couples. Another aspect of their work is visiting schools to talk to young people about the beauty and dignity of the life commitment that is the Sacrament of Marriage. We need to avail of opportunities to celebrate marriage in the Church. Many parishes bring together each year those celebrating silver and golden anniversaries and those married in the past year, to recognise and celebrate the beauty that is the gift of married fidelity 'for richer, for poorer, in sickness or in health' over all the years.

The wedding is a beautiful ceremony full of symbolism and ritual. It gathers a community and a family in the 'Joy of Love'. But it can also be a time of immense stress and even greater expense for a couple starting out. Sadly, some couples I know have put off getting married for this very reason. One feels that couples are exploited on their wedding day because everything related to the wedding is more expensive than the norm. Yet on the other hand, there is a deep desire in families that this will be a special day to remember, regardless of expense. Pope Francis' says

'Have courage to be different. What is important is the love you share … you are capable of opting for a more modest and simple celebration in which love takes precedence over everything else'. This will really take a lot of courage and freedom in the context of today's wedding culture. Again in Ireland, we see more and more couples opting for a civil ceremony. We must never make these couples feel less welcome when they may come to church for other weddings, funerals or family events.

At every wedding ceremony, both single and married people stand side by stand. On these occasions they are open to the beauty and wonder that this sacred celebration holds. We can use this occasion to celebrate the beautiful sacrament with prayerful solemnity and with a warm humanity that can touch the hearts of young couples who may be contemplating this life commitment in the coming years. Wedding expenses are largely accrued as a result of the lavish wedding reception rather than the ceremony itself. But the Church must continually distinguish the beautiful simplicity that is the essence of the sacrament from the trappings that can sometimes take over, bringing with it the burden of expense and debt. Sadly, sometimes, the trappings of the wedding day can take from the meaning, that is, the life commitment of the marriage sacrament.

We live in a culture where life commitment has a shaky foundation. However, there is still something extraordinary about the couple who stand before each other, make a promise and give their word to be true and faithful to each other in life 'until death do us part'. It takes immense courage, trust, faith and hope in the other and in oneself. In the words of the exhortation, 'Honouring God's word, fidelity to one's promises; these are things that cannot be bought and sold. They cannot be compelled by force or maintained without sacrifice' (*AL*, 214). That is why at every wedding I witness I know I stand on sacred ground. Despite all their fears and fragility, the couple promises to be the face of God for each other – to be there for each other for life; to not give up or let go or walk away, but to stay together and pray for each other. It needs the constant support of friends and the extended family. I can't help but notice the importance of life-long friends. The best man or bridesmaid is often the friend they made in primary school, and remains a friend for life.

And so the couple sets out on the journey of life together. But it is a work in progress – a life-long project. The beautiful haunting phrase that Francis uses to stop the relationship becoming 'stagnant': 'Young love needs to keep dancing towards the future with immense hope …' (*AL,* 219). Love is a work of art. Love allows each to wait for the other with the patience of an artist – a patience that comes from God. The couple are called to create or recreate each other and help each other to be the best they can be. Together, as parents, they are called to 'create new life' with 'tenderness and authentic freedom'. This is the beautiful ideal and in the children, the couple, as new parents, can forge even deeper bonds of trust and mutual support. To look at the parents' face as they hold their new-born baby at Baptism is to see a reflection of the face of God. It is a love, that more than anything, reflects the loving gaze of God, full of tenderness and the Joy of Love. The creation of their baby 'creates parents'. It creates new levels of awareness; it creates a space in the heart they did not know existed. This is a sad paradox, that in a time when there is a clamour for greater access to abortion, there were never more couples longing to be blessed by the gift of new life. Perhaps it is because many couples start a family much later in life. In a time where the handicapped child is seen as a burden, I have witnessed again and again the power of such a child to transform parents and bring extraordinary grace as well as deep peace to parents and their family. Our callous world needs these special gifted children to help us discover love in its most pure form again and to take from us our hearts of stone.

Dealing with Stresses

There are so many pressures and crisis points on a family today. The pace of life, the pressure of work, lack of time together, all place a strain on the couple. There is an urgent need for families to make time for each other. As Pope Francis says, 'Love needs time and space, everything else is secondary' (*AL, 244*). We need to create moments of closeness through daily rituals, playing games, sitting around the table for a family meal, telling stories, sharing household chores, birthdays and anniversaries. Sometimes we forget the beauty of the ordinary and the everyday. When a partner dies I notice it is always the simple rituals of shared kindnesses that the bereaved partner misses the most. 'As long as we can celebrate, we are able to rekindle our love, to free it from monotony and to colour our daily routine with hope' (*AL, 226*). For bereaved people it often proves to be helpful to bring people together who have shared the same journey of loss. Those who are further along the road can help those who are setting out on this heart-breaking 'Camino' of loss and bereavement. In a similar way for families, we could have family days and a family mass where groups of parents meet to come up with practical suggestions for celebrating family life, and involve the children and young people in the celebrations. The 'Play and Pray' initiative is a very good way to make the Sunday Liturgy speak to the hearts of little children as they are taken out during the Liturgy of the Word to play and pray the Word of God for that day.

Praying as a family can nurture faith, heal wounds and foster a spirituality in the family. This is not easy. Since the family Rosary is no longer prayed together we seem to be at a loss as to how to pray as a family. As Irish people, we seem to be very self-conscious about praying together. Creating and engaging with the sacred space encouraged in the sacramental preparation of our children might help. The children can lead us in their prayer with the simplicity of innocence and their Bible stories. Such prayer can help us to learn how to listen to each other with the ear of the heart in the face of family crisis and conflicts, thus keeping alive the fire that is the Joy of Love.

Separation and divorce are at times inevitable in the face of violence, abuse and the complete breakdown in communication. This is especially painful for those who are most vulnerable as they usually have fewer resources, financial or psychological, to help them to rebuild their lives. Such a person is deeply wounded by violence or betrayal. They can easily feel misjudged or less worthy if they enter a new relationship. We must be very careful not to add an extra burden of guilt but go out of our way to make them always feel welcome and at home in our Church. Most often, it is the children who bear the deepest scars. Children can easily be used as pawns in family conflict. But in truth, I know many parents in such circumstances who never speak ill of the other partner in front of their children. They continue to try to create some form of stability in a very difficult and delicate relationship. One of the most poignant experiences for me is to watch the separated parents of the bride or groom on a wedding day. They sit beside each other in the church unable to speak or communicate, unable to fully share the beauty of this special family day. Sometimes such couples can be helped by the sensitive counselling of ACCORD, to heal deep hurts and resentments of the past. The priest can be seen as

Christ's face of Compassion that seeks always to make those who are wounded by the past at home and welcome in our church. Such people must never feel judged or less loved.

Finally, the exhortation speaks of the delicate areas in family life, including mixed marriages and same-sex attraction. Gay people may sometimes feel judged and less accepted in a Church that celebrates the uniqueness of the heterosexual relationship of marriage. Gay and lesbian people have many gifts to enrich the life of the Church. At all times we should celebrate, welcome and value their contribution and, needless to say, value them as individuals uniquely created and beautiful in the eyes of God.

Equally a mixed marriage is a living ecumenical experience. Whether the marriage is with a person from another Christian denomination or a person of another faith, every opportunity should be availed of to include the partner that is not Catholic and to make them feel at ease in the parish church and parish celebrations. Opportunities, such as the Week of Prayer for Christian Unity, might be used in order to help a couple share their personal experience of living in a 'mixed marriage' and rearing their children in such a religious environment. In all such cases the language of the exhortation is sensitive, understanding and keen to reflect 'the attitude of the Lord Jesus who offers his boundless love to each person without exception' (AL, 250). Would that this was the case in the past. Would that this could always be the case today. The Church must try to speak with the voice of God to the children of his love. The tone, as well as the words used, should always be of kindness and understanding.

Death is a great wound of the soul. The death of a spouse or the death of a child is a pain that is beyond words and sometimes beyond tears. In a tragic death I have experienced again and again the most dignified and heroic courage and the ability to think of others. At times like this, the extended family comes into their own in support. Neighbours and the parish community respond in ways that show the most compassionate face of a community. After some time this network of support may lessen. In my experience, therefore, a group of other parents or spouses who have experienced such a loss can be of the greatest and most sustained support for the bereaved person.

To give families time, to listen to them with the 'ear of the heart', is a grace given and a much greater grace received. Such an experience often brings me to a place of silence and prayer. This is a sacred place of the heart where God lives forever as endless compassion in the home of the family. This is indeed the 'Gospel of the family'. This is indeed the Word made flesh. This is indeed the Joy of Love.

Reflection Questions

1. 'The Irish families who have no home, the refugee camps of desperate people without a home or a homeland, are the cries in the wilderness seeking compassionate and generous hospitality, a place to call home.' How should individuals, families and parishes respond to this call?

2. 'It is important that the training of seminarians be grounded in and guided by the reality, beauty and complexity of family life today.' How could this become a practical reality?

3. Is there any way in which parishes could foster a culture of modest but beautiful celebration of marriage as a corrective to the culture of massive expenditure on wedding days?

4. 'Gay and lesbian people have many gifts to enrich the life of the Church. At all times we should celebrate, welcome and value their contribution and, needless to say, to value them as individuals uniquely created and beautiful in the eyes of God.' How can this be done in practical ways, without compromising core values presented again in *Amoris Laetitia*?

Some Pastoral Perspectives

DEIRDRE O'RAWE

A pastoral perspective is not an abstract understanding of God but a response that is alive and shapes and forms everyday experience. In other words, when we interact with others from a pastoral perspective we do so with the compassion, love and mercy of Jesus. This is how we build up God's Kingdom on earth and make God's face visible in the world.

Through Baptism we are all, ordained and lay, called to play our part in the building up of the Kingdom of God on earth. The parish community, using the gifts and talents of its members has an important role. The family, the basic unit of society, is a primary target group for pastoral support. By supporting the family, Christian marriage is also being supported. It is the mission of the Church to do this. Establishment of God's Kingdom on earth was Jesus' dream for the world. It was his mission, as He lived among us in his physical body. It is his mission today too as he lives among us in his mystical body, the Church. Parish is the basic community of the Church's hierarchical structure and the foundational building block of community is the family.

Parish: A Co-responsible Community

Parish is the cutting edge of where the great mystery that is the Church exercises its mission as the instrument of salvation. The parish community is the family of God working within the fabric of human society. It is an evangelising agent, proclaiming the presence of God in the world, with the emphasis on Gospel values and attitudes. As such, it supports couples who chose to marry in our Church and enables them in the process of passing down the faith to their children. This requires catechesis, self-reflection and discernment. It is about building Christian community by targeting the foundational building block which is the family. To accomplish this, the priest and laity have to work together co-responsibly, where every member is active and using her or his gifts and talents in continuing Christ's work of redemption. Central to the success of this vision of parish, where priest and laity work together co-responsibly, is the formation of a properly formed and informed pastoral council. A properly *formed* pastoral council has a mindset that has moved away from the concept of collaboration, namely that the lay person is helping the priest, to taking ownership of his or her own baptismal commitment. A properly *informed* pastoral council has moved away from the vision of Church as *institution* to the vision of Church as *community*. The RCIA process, which has a strong emphasis on the Sacraments of Initiation, lends itself ably to the realisation of this formation and information. Through this process, parish pastoral councils come to have a vision of Church which is fit for purpose. Indeed, I might suggest that it would be obligatory for those who are called to be members of their parish pastoral council, together with their priest, to follow the RCIA process. After all, that would be no different to what Jesus did with those he called to carry on his mission when he would no longer be on earth. He formed and informed them. The people he chose were simple, ordinary uneducated people. One of the great characteristics of those he called was that they were teachable. Through his teaching he could write his message on their hearts. He shaped them and made them fit for the purpose of carrying on his mission of building God's Kingdom on earth.

Supporting Marriage

I mentioned above the importance of supporting family and marriage. When a marriage fails it has a negative impact on the family and society. Good preparation of couples for the Sacrament of Marriage is a must. The increasing secularisation of society poses a challenge for those involved in the ministry of preparation for the Sacrament of Marriage. In their Guidelines for the Preparation of Couples for Marriage (2016), the Catholic Bishops' Conference of England and Wales[1] state:

> For many couples approaching the Church to be married, this may be their first experience (since school) of the Church's pastoral concern for their future happiness. It may also be their first opportunity to begin to learn of God's love and care for them, to see in their own love story, the love story of God for his people and from all that, their own part in the story of salvation, passing on faith in God to the next generation.

A good experience of marriage preparation can also lay the foundations for a fruitful relationship to develop between the couple and the parish, enabling the couple to accept the parish as an *extended family* to which they can turn in times of joy and sorrow, in times of challenge and opportunity. There is a growing awareness that good marriages and healthy families don't happen just by chance but as a result of working together to create a secure and loving environment. The properly *formed* and *informed* pastoral council working co-responsibly with the priest has to form a ministry for the family in the parish that would specifically focus on the well-being of couples and their children.

We are constantly reminded of the importance of education, prevention and early intervention in all areas of life. This is particularly true when embarking on the most important and biggest commitment of a lifetime. To love is to choose and this may not be difficult when life is going according to plan. Commitment can be difficult when life is a struggle. The parish community should strive to support couples so that they can remain committed to each other through all the stages of marriage; committed to their spouses on the good days, committed to their marriages on the difficult days and committed to their commitment on the days when it seems impossible. Married couples are ideally placed in a parish to become mentors to engaged couples and newlyweds. They can welcome couples into the parish and a cup of tea afterwards helps build community and is an ideal opportunity for getting to know families. Child-friendly Sunday worship and special liturgies for marriage and family bring people together and an evening of reflection and prayer can help couples discern their vocation as married couples. The parish pastoral council should ensure that they have up to date information to direct families to diocesan or state agencies which can help in times of need.

In the Catholic faith, marriage is a sacrament and for couples their commitment to marriage is an important part of their witness to their faith. Couples preparing for this sacrament are invited to reflect on this commitment, how they communicate and manage conflict, their family of origin and hopes for a family of their own, their role in the parish and wider Church. For this reason, significant numbers of couples opt for the faith-based provision, ACCORD, the Catholic marriage care service that facilitates preparation for the Sacrament of Marriage. Marriage preparation helps the man and woman to prepare each other for *their* marriage. Essentially, it is about beginning a conversation that will continue throughout the married life of the couple. The real experts in any relationship are the couple themselves. An understanding of the grace they will receive on their wedding day and a grace they can ask for daily, is at the heart of an ACCORD course. It is this grace that will sustain them when life deals a hand that is hard to play.

One could argue that effective marriage preparation should eliminate the need for counselling; if only life were that simple. When couples give their consent and exchange their vows, they can never know what life holds for them. Couples/individuals coming for counselling are often distressed and experiencing communication difficulties, conflict, domestic abuse, financial pressures, childcare and family stresses, intimacy issues, infidelity, addiction and sexual issues. In ACCORD, professionally trained pastoral counsellors help individuals and couples to develop new insights about themselves and their relationship, manage conflict and other challenges in a constructive manner. The objective is always to support their relationship and bring the ensuing benefits to their children and family life. The Church must always provide a safe space for couples to talk and listen. In this intimate space, hope can be restored, healing can begin and love can grow again.

Faith-based organisations have a wealth of experience and effective practice to draw on. Many have been supporting families throughout life stages and have gained invaluable experience and knowledge of 'family' in the communities in which they serve. They have a long history of providing care and support to families, including vital services for the most vulnerable and marginalised. Based in local communities, these networks can provide a holistic approach to supporting and strengthening families. Families face many challenges today and we are ever mindful that Church teaching emphasises both the responsibility of policy makers to protect the family, and the responsibility of the Church to advocate policies that support family life and challenge laws or structures that infringe upon or deny the rights and dignity of families. Church-based volunteers make a vital contribution to addressing need in this area. The word 'volunteer' has a Latin ancestor: *voluntarius*, meaning 'of one's free will'; being free to serve, to listen, to accept the moral responsibilities and spiritual rewards that accompany a calling to serve. These lay ministers are the custodians of what Pope Francis calls, 'the fundamental pillars that govern a nation … the *family*, the foundation of coexistence and a remedy against social fragmentation.'[2] In a Christian sense, service is a gift, an opportunity to express generosity and compassion, sympathy and support, an opportunity to realise love.

The celebration of a wedding in Church is a divine occasion; a reminder to all couples present of their own happy wedding days, and an occasion for them to pray for God's blessing again on their own marriages. Marriage is a step into the unknown and couples can take that step with confidence because, since their marriage is a sacrament, they know God is going to be with them every step of the way. That is why we describe marriage in the Catholic Church as a sacrament. It is a covenant; a solemn vow between a man and a woman and God. In those times when love and joy, peace and harmony – the hallmarks of Christian marriage – get a bit frayed, couples will have the grace of God, that power from on high, to enable them to accept and forgive each other. The Holy Spirit will give them the graces they need to encourage each other, to share feelings, emotions and passions, hopes and fears, resentments and disappointments, ups and downs.

The School of Marriage

Of course, a couple cannot know when they stand before the altar, give their consent and exchange solemn vows, what life will hold. The wedding lasts only one day, but marriage is for the rest of their lives. On the wedding day, the couple go back to school again, the school of marriage. They begin to learn again, to learn to love each other in a deeper way. As Catholics, we believe we go horizontally to God through the ministry of the Church. Husbands and wives go to God through one another. As Church, we must try to equip couples with the skills to enable them to do that. ACCORD provides an opportunity for couples (Catholic and inter-church) to look at how they communicate, and learn the vital skills of how to make the face of God visible to one another, to their children and in their neighbourhoods. Some couples coming on a course may not be aware of how they communicate and what is unhelpful in a heated discussion. Using practical exercises, ACCORD facilitators help them to focus on how to communicate effectively and how to avoid 'pinch' situations turning into 'crunch' dilemmas. Course evaluations show that for many future spouses, this may be the first time they have heard the other express his or her feelings in certain situations. With this new awareness couples can begin to open up to each other more and experience a closeness that binds, protects and nourishes.

Forgiveness and seeking to understand the other's weaknesses and excuse them isn't always easy. Effective marriage preparation will focus on commitment, communication, dealing with conflict, and parenthood but always through the prism of family of origin. Couples planning to marry ought to be aware of what they have learned in their first home. For some, it may be that as children they picked up messages that were unhelpful or even damaging. Unlearning these messages is important so that each of them can become the person God wants them to be. Sometimes being distant, avoiding affection and being fearful in our closest relationships has to do with our not being able to accept ourselves, our limitations and even to forgive ourselves. If we accept that God's love is unconditional then we will be able to show love and forgive others – even if they have wronged us. To be able to forgive comes from the experience of understanding and forgiving ourselves. Often it is the most fragile part that bears the fruit. In marriage, spouses have the privilege of knowing and loving each other in a unique way that can help heal wounds and instil hope.

The marriage relationship can be, for most people, their chief means of personal fulfilment and salvation. When marriage relationships break down the parish is committed to stay with the couple, believing that God never abandons his people. As parish communities, our primary mission is to come alongside, to meet people where they are at, to travel in their direction, however inconvenient. Parish-based initiatives can be a vital source of support for lone parents and their children who are among those most at risk of poverty and related problems of loneliness and isolation; to enter into their stories, pain, joys, to identify with them, to listen intently, to be fully present. The important thing is to find Jesus challenging us to love, to have compassion, to practice justice, to live in freedom, to be able to forgive and be reconciled, to be kind, gentle and accepting, to seek to find and to respond to him in all things.

Some priests may find it difficult to reconcile a pastoral response with the teaching of the Church. Undoubtedly, there are situations where this will be challenging. Priests will need the wisdom of their bishop and fellow priests to reflect and discern on what Pope Francis is saying in this exhortation. Hospitality, accompaniment, discernment, integration and conversion are stages on the journey for a couple who find themselves 'outside' Church. Accompanying a couple is not something the priest is called to do alone. The support of the bishop in teasing out complex situations and considering a pastoral solution is critical. Pastoral councils have much to offer in creating a welcoming, inclusive environment and helping couples on this journey to integration. Formation of priests and laity is a lifelong process and we need each other for understanding, wisdom, perseverance and guidance. This quest is never-ending and it involves a deep commitment, a willingness to *learn* and unlearn, to *pray*, to *share*, to *search*, in order to respond to the variety of human needs we encounter. Ongoing catechesis, prayer and training are the essential ingredients so that it is always the Holy Spirit who is setting the agenda.

Amoris Laetitia is an inspiration to organisations such as ACCORD and pastoral councils, which strive to facilitate better understanding and reconciliation, to enable couples to realise a new future for themselves, and hopefully find in their relationships freedom from antagonism, disappointment, anger, and fear. The 'art of accompaniment', according to Pope Francis, can teach us 'to remove our sandals before the sacred ground of the other'. There are times in any relationship when such a seemingly simple gesture can become complicated, and the Church must be there to prepare and support couples both before they marry, and at times when their journey together becomes complicated. Surely, if the 'art of accompaniment' can lead us anywhere, it is to the rediscovery of hope.

Reflection Questions

1. This section calls for all members of a parish pastoral council, along with their priest/s, to follow the RCIA process. The Synod on the Family asked for a new 'marriage catechumenate', where couples would be formed for marriage within the context of the parish community, with their priest and mentor couples working together, guiding them before the wedding and after, when they take their first steps as a new family. How could this operate in a practical way in parishes? (This article from the National Catholic Register may help. http://bit.ly/2lJVo1G)

2. 'On the wedding day, the couple go back to school again, the school of marriage. They begin to learn again, to learn to love each other in a deeper way.' How prevalent is this view of marriage in the Catholic community, do you think?

3. This section emphasises partnership between priests and laypeople. Are there places where you have seen this work very well in relation to family life in a parish?

4. 'Some priests may find it difficult to reconcile a pastoral response with the teaching of the Church. Undoubtedly, there are situations where this will be challenging.' What are the most challenging situations? Are you aware of situations where a sensitive response has managed to balance pastoral needs with the teaching of the Church?

Endnotes

1. *Guidelines for the Preparation of Couples for Marriage*, Department for Christian Responsibility & Citizenship, Catholic Bishops' Conference of England & Wales, Rejoice Publications, 2016
2. http://w2.vatican.va/content/francesco/en/speeches/2013/july/documents/papa-francesco_20130725_gmg-comunita-varginha.html Par 2

Chapter Seven

Towards a Better Education of Children

KATE LIFFEY

The Beautiful Everyday

On a recent trip to the cinema with my two little girls, I was very taken by the fun animated film, *Trolls*. Princess Poppy was the heroine who, following her father's example, sought to ensure in a situation of real danger for the whole Troll family that 'no troll was left behind'! The film was a quirky, tuneful exploration of the themes of friendship, family, solidarity and 'going the extra mile' because of love.

I was equally taken by two advertisements shown before the film. The first, with the tagline, 'the beautiful everyday', was from a well-known Scandinavian furniture company. This series of advertisements is designed to get people thinking about how we live at home and as families. The advertisement brilliantly and movingly captures the love between a mother and her son. The second one was for baby wipes. It opens with a father's hand gently stroking a tiny new-born baby's face. This close-up shot then moves to a mother holding her new-born baby to her chest. The advertisement is cleverly designed to demonstrate the strength of the deep attachment between parent and baby.

There is something so powerful and yet so very simple about the core relationships presented in these advertisements, in the film and at the heart of every family. As Bishop Brendan Leahy points out in his book on rediscovering family today, *Dreaming Big; Living the Reality*,[1] 'there is nostalgia in every human heart for the family', and as humans 'we yearn for the feeling of family.'

When filmmakers and marketing people tap into the power and simplicity of family, they present it as a universal good to which we can all feel connected.

In exploring the family in *Amoris Laetitia,* Pope Francis uncovers for us the qualities of familial love and presence that these two beautiful ads exemplify. Pope Francis digs deep into the ordinary reality of family life, the 'lights and shadows' (*AL,* 32) and through this digging demonstrates clearly that the 'everyday', in terms of family, is very beautiful indeed and can teach us so much about who we are, and ultimately who God is.

A Broad Tapestry

As a mother of three children – aged six and under – I have engaged with *Amoris Laetitia* primarily through the lens of my own experience as a mother to Tess, Maeve and Robert and wife to Geoff. I also read it in the context of being a very busy working mother heavily reliant on my excellent child-minder, my parents and wider family for help and support.

In my slow reading and re-reading of the text, I have learned a great deal about parenting, marriage, faith, love and ultimately about why family matters. I have also read it as a teacher and catechist and it is at the intersection of these two spaces that I have been asking myself the question: what specifically does *Amoris Laetitia* tell us about education in the family?

Chapter seven, 'Towards a Better Education of Children', is an obvious starting point, but simply going to that chapter and reading it will not uncover all of the richness of what Pope Francis has to say about education. *Amoris Laetitia* may well be accessible in terms of the language Pope Francis uses but it is not a simple document in terms of what he is trying to teach about a whole range of issues, including education.

While Pope Francis in his introduction acknowledges that certain chapters might be more useful to married couples, to parents or to pastors, we must be careful to avoid the temptation towards any over-simplification of the message or to an unhelpful instrumentalisation of its contents, that is, extracting pieces of text that might be deemed useful in support of a particular position or approach. Instead, the whole of *Amoris Laetitia* might be most appropriately read in terms of an almost encyclopaedic expression of the Church's teaching on so many different aspects of marriage and family. Maybe even more importantly, the document should be read in the context of a rich expression of the beautiful spirituality of love and mercy that underpins that teaching. Pope Francis himself cautions against a rushed reading of the text. The entire document is about education; specifically, what it is we should be learning and teaching one another in the Church about family, our world, faith and the God of Love. Pope Francis is a catechist; a teacher of the faith and it is in that context that everything he writes, says and does might be best understood.

It is also useful to keep in mind what Pope Francis has written and said about education in previous documents and contexts, such as *Laudato Si': On the Care of our Common Home* and also in *Evangelii Gaudium* (the Joy of the Gospel). *Misericordiae Vultus*, the Bull of Indiction for the Year of Mercy, also clearly speaks to the goals and purpose of all education, but particularly education in the faith. There is a 'back and forth' required in our reading of *Amoris Laetitia* between, in particular, *Evangelii Gaudium* and *Laudato Si'* to ensure the richest possible understanding of what Pope Francis is saying about family and marriage in general and education in particular.

Another important way of avoiding any limited instrumentalisation of the text is to try first to understand what Pope Francis is saying about God's love for God's people and for the world in which we live. The 'sister' chapter to chapter seven on education might well be chapter nine on the spirituality of marriage and the family. There is a rich affective and spiritual engagement required with what Pope Francis says about love, faith, and God if we are to make sense of what he says in particular about education.

Key to that affective and spiritual engagement, are the two words 'joy' and 'tenderness'. In *Evangelii Gaudium* and in *Amoris Laetitia*, Pope Francis puts 'joy' centre stage and not just in the titles of both. He tells us that in the family we find an icon of God's love for us and it is that reality of God's love in the heart of our families that brings joy to the world and to the Church. The family is not just a social construct, or even just a place where education of children should happen. For Pope Francis, it is part of God's plan for humanity because in the family, through love, we come into intimate, life-giving, challenging contact with the God who is Love. In both documents, and in *Misericordiae Vultus*, he invites us into an understanding of our God who is all mercy and compassion; slow to anger and rich in mercy. He uses the image of a mother holding her baby to her breast and suggests that it is in this incredibly beautiful and close relationship that we see the face of God. Any exploration of the theme of education makes sense only in an understanding of a God who invites us to experience the pure joy of knowing what it is to be loved by him. And of course, for Pope Francis, that 'knowing' begins in the heart of every family, in the wonderful ordinariness of everyday life together.

By way of an example, we can think of tenderness in the context of the unborn child. Pope Francis, in three very beautiful paragraphs in *Amoris Laetitia* encourages expectant mothers to dream about their babies (*AL*, 169) and not to allow themselves to be 'robbed of the interior joy of motherhood … Ask the Lord to preserve your joy, so that you can pass it on to your child' (*AL*, 171). All children, he tells us in chapter five, 'Love Made Fruitful', are also held in love and joy by God, our heavenly Father. Because 'every child growing within the mother's womb is part of the eternal loving plan of God the Father: ... Each child has a place in God's heart from all eternity; once he or she is conceived, the Creator's eternal dream comes true' (*AL*, 168). When we understand our children in this way – as pure gift held so tenderly in our heavenly Father's heart for all eternity – it changes everything. And, in particular, of course, it changes what and how we wish to teach them. Within this very broad tapestry and particularly within the context of the rich spirituality flowing into and from the Joy of Love, how might we then begin to explore what Francis has to say specifically about education in *Amoris Laetitia*?

No Stereotype of the Ideal Family

As a second level religious education teacher I was taught that the first lesson in teaching is to 'know your audience'! And so this is where we must also begin. Pope Francis tells us in chapter two that 'we would do well to focus on concrete realities'; the 'beautiful ordinary' of that cinema advertisement. He tells us that it is 'through these realities that the Church can be guided to a more profound understanding of the inexhaustible mystery of marriage and the family' (*AL*, 31). The experience of family in all its complexity comes first; and from that the Church engages with, learns from, supports, and celebrates with families. In *Evangelii Gaudium* he also tells us that realities are more important than ideas; and that this principle calls us to reject 'the various means of masking reality', including '... objectives more ideal than real ... ethical systems bereft of kindness, intellectual discourse bereft of wisdom' (*EG*, 231). The 'inexhaustible mystery of marriage and family' explored throughout *Amoris Laetitia* is centred on the 'lights and shadows' of family and on the simple truth that, as the synod was clearly at pains to point out, 'there is no stereotype of the ideal family, but rather a challenging mosaic made up of many different realities, with all their joys, hopes and problems'. Father Eamonn Conway and Cathal Barry in their useful study guide on *Amoris Laetitia*[2] list sixteen different challenges explored by Pope Francis in chapter two. No two families are the same. There needs to be an acknowledgement that any very particular 'one-size-fits-all' propositions are very unlikely to succeed in any meaningful or sustainable way. We have to meet every family where they are by listening to their stories, engaging with compassion with their realities, and giving them the necessary disposition and tools to teach and learn.

An Integral Education: Where and For What Purpose?

Where does Pope Francis see education happening? His primary focus is on the family and not on schools. Education in the context of school is mentioned, but primarily regarding the role of the school in assisting parents to fulfil their duties. This advice, Leonardi Franchi suggests is 'particularly needed in countries where the state is seeking to gain increasing power over families and the rearing of children'. Franchi tells us that 'Francis is not downplaying the role of the school but calling for parents to take their responsibility as 'first educators' seriously, and reminding education professionals that they must work with not against the family.[3]

What is Pope Francis saying is the purpose of this education? In chapter seven he reminds us that 'the family is the primary setting for socialisation since it is there that we first learn to relate to others, to listen and share, to be patient and show respect, to help one another and live as one.' (*AL, 276*) This is at the heart of Pope Francis's understanding of what an 'integral' education might look like. It isn't something that can be compartmentalised. It happens every day in families in a whole host of different ways and contexts. It is simply what families do.

He goes on to say that the task of education is to: make us sense that the world and society are also our home; it trains us how to live together in this greater home. In the family, we learn closeness, care and respect for others ... We come to realise that we are living with and alongside others who are worthy of our concern, our kindness and our affection. (*AL, 276*) He is concerned primarily with attitudes and habits and sees the role of parents as being to help to form and develop both. The family is the school of good living, where children learn in very simple ways the disposition and skills required to live with others within the family, within local communities and as global citizens. They are educated in love, in hope, in patience, and in sensitivity (particularly in relation to human frailty and illness). This is also an integral education; helping children realise that we are all one.

This is echoed strongly in *Laudato Si'* when Pope Francis tells us that 'we need to strengthen the conviction that we are one single human family' (*LS, 52*). Of the family's role in ecological education, he says:

> In the family, we first learn how to show love and respect for life; we are taught the proper use of things, order and cleanliness, respect for the local ecosystem and care for all creatures. In the family, we receive an integral education, which enables us to grow harmoniously in personal maturity. (*LS, 213*)

At the heart of this 'integral education' (*AL*, 156) is, of course, a particular spirituality. The person, as we learn in chapter five, is a part of God's eternal dream. An integral education seeks to teach children that we are called to respect all human life from conception to natural death. It also seeks to teach our children the importance of caring, in particular, for the most vulnerable among us; the sick, the elderly, the poor, refugees and migrants and those who are on the margins for a whole range of different reasons.

This is a spirituality that also speaks to the ultimate end or purpose of education. At the end of chapter seven, Pope Francis offers a superb summary of the ultimate purpose of education in the family when he writes, 'All of us should be able to say, thanks to the experience of our life in the family: "We come to believe in the love that God has for us"' (1 Jn 4:16). This coming to a deep awareness of the love God has for each of us is at the heart of all education in the family. Not surprisingly then, the question, 'What is love?' is core to any exploration of education in the family. Chapter four also provides us with a really beautiful answer to this question that so many of us ask, 'What is love?' While the focus of chapter four is very much on 'Love in Marriage', what Pope Francis writes here is for the whole family because such 'love is experienced and nurtured in the daily life of couples and their children' (*AL*, 90).

In this chapter and elsewhere Pope Francis makes clear that the ultimate human vocation is to love and it is in the family that we can best learn such love. It is in the family that we learn first that we are not alone and that no one should feel alone or lonely. Chapter four also shows us what exactly the love that needs to be taught to children might look like; that it is patient, at the service of others, not jealous, not boastful, not rude, is generous, is not irritable or resentful, that it forgives, that love rejoices with others, that it bears all things, believes all things, hopes all things and that love endures all things (cf. 1 Cor 13: 4-7). This very beautiful, consoling and realistic chapter highlights just how significant the challenges are for parents and for families.

In the very last paragraph of *Amoris Laetitia* we learn that 'this is a never-ending vocation born of the full communion of the Trinity, the profound unity between Christ and his Church, the loving community which is the Holy Family of Nazareth, and the pure fraternity existing among the saints of heaven' (*AL*, 325). Family is the place where we can learn to cry out, like St Thérèse of Lisieux, 'O Jesus, my Love, at last I have found my vocation, my vocation is Love!' Not surprisingly at all then, Pope Francis reiterates the central role of the family both for the Church and for society as a whole (*AL*, 87), and reminds us of the need for families to receive adequate care, protection, and pastoral support.

What are the qualities of an integral education in the home?

a) Patient Realism

In chapter seven, and in much of the rest of the document, Pope Francis prioritises what he describes as 'patient realism'. Similar to 'the real being more important than ideas', he also suggests that 'time is greater than space' (*EG*, 222–225; *AL*, 261). In the moral and ethical education of children that of necessity precedes and provides the foundation for a more explicit education in the faith, Pope Francis advocates demanding from children 'only a degree of effort that will not lead to resentment or coercion' (*AL*, 271). This, he says, is done 'by proposing small steps that can be understood, accepted and appreciated' (*AL*, 271). He also feels that adolescents should be educated in moral education in a similarly patient and realistic way. He says 'we have to proceed slowly, taking into consideration the child's age and abilities, without presuming to apply rigid and inflexible methods'. (*AL,* 273)

As a mother, prone to the inevitable very human worries that come with being a parent, I find this hugely consoling. Reading this very simple, grounded advice reminds that that in the context of, for example, my feisty five-year-old's difficulties settling into 'big' school – a month in, and we'd already been called in to see the teacher – I have to learn to trust not only my child but also myself and my husband. More than that, I have to learn (and re-learn) to trust in the love God has for her as his beloved daughter and for us as her parents. Pope Francis reminds us that 'this means that we need to ask God to act in their hearts, in places where we ourselves cannot reach'. (*AL,* 287)

Such trust in God's love is not an easy 'out' for parents! Correction is essential because correction is 'also an incentive whenever children's efforts are appreciated and acknowledged, and they sense their parents' constant, patient trust' (*AL,* 269). However, all correction takes place in the context of the love in the family and the trust the child has built up through his/her parents' love. It also takes place in the context of a rich prayer life and entrusts our children to their heavenly father who loves them and wants them to have life and have it to the full.

Similarly, Pope Francis emphasises the need for sex education which he says can only be 'seen within the broader framework of an education for love; for mutual self-giving' (*AL,* 280). The language of the body, he says, 'calls for a patient apprenticeship in learning to interpret and channel desires in view of authentic self-giving' (*AL,* 284). In these paragraphs, there is a significant emphasis on discovering new ways of teaching 'old' virtues like discipline, modesty, and respect that meet the challenges of our time.

b) Being Present and Being Attentive

At the heart of this patient realism lies an awareness from parents of where their children are; not only physically but perhaps, even more importantly, where they are on their journey in life. At the start of chapter seven, he stresses the importance of spending time with our children, listening to them, talking to them and sharing with them our own experiences and learnings. This is not 'helicopter parenting', however. Instead, he says, 'what is most important is the ability lovingly to help them grow in freedom, maturity, overall discipline and real autonomy' (*AL,* 261). Knowing where our children are 'existentially' encourages what Pope Francis calls 'the responsible use of freedom to face issues with good sense and intelligence' (*AL,* 262).

In typically pragmatic fashion, Pope Francis cautions in particular against the unwise use of technology in families. Real presence in families, born of the kind of tenderness at the heart of a mother or father's relationship with their child, means that we attend to one another with great care and as completely as we can. In a very beautiful passage in chapter nine, he writes, 'It is a profound spiritual experience to contemplate our loved ones with the eyes of God and to see Christ in them' (*AL,* 323). He tells us that our loved ones merit our complete attention. Anything that causes a 'technological disconnect', that breaks into the kind of attention our children need and deserve, should to be carefully controlled because 'we cannot ignore the risks that these new forms of communication pose for children and adolescents; at times they can foster apathy and disconnect from the real world' (*AL,* 278). The challenge for parents is not just to teach their children about making real connections in the here and now. They themselves must model this kind of attention.

Again, underpinning the call to be really present to our children is the call to tenderness. In chapter nine on the spirituality of marriage and the family, there is a rich exploration of the notion of Christ's presence dwelling 'in real and concrete families, with all their daily troubles and struggles' (*AL*, 315). In this context, 'the spirituality of family love is made up of thousands of small but real gestures' (*AL*, 315). How we attune ourselves to these spirit-filled gestures is the key to understanding Pope Francis's teaching in chapter seven on 'passing on the faith'.

c) Forming our children in the faith

Pope Francis leaves faith formation within the family to the very end of chapter seven, and wisely provides very little in terms of specific pathways. This is unsurprising given that what of necessity underpins faith formation, happens in the other kinds of learning that occur in families; learning centred in particular on the development of good habits and on the ethical development of children.

As in *Evangelii Gaudium*, Pope Francis points to the evangelising power of popular piety (cf. *EG*, 122–126) and simple devotion (*AL*, 288). Life is so busy, sometimes the best (and indeed only) way of teaching our children about God is in and through those little gestures; those 'actions, symbols and stories' (*AL*, 288) that can be woven into everyday life. For me as a mother, what I am trying to do is to help my children grow in a deep appreciation of the 'meaning and beauty of the faith'. (*AL*, 287) This means developing my children's spiritual imagination and affectivity. This is not done artificially through one or two catechetical moments a day; it needs to happen throughout the day. It happens naturally when you are attuned to your own faith and to God's Spirit moving in and through your family and in the world around you. It also happens as Pope Francis advises by being 'sensitive to your child's patterns of growth' (*AL*, 288); that patient and attentive realism again.

As in *Evangelii Gaudium*, *Laudato Si'*, and *Misericordiae Vultus*, Pope Francis points to the ultimate goal of such faith formation in families. We are called to make real the love of God through, 'solidarity with the poor, openness to a diversity of people, the protection of creation, commitment to the transformation of unjust social structures' (*AL,* 290) and through the practice of the corporal and spiritual works of mercy 'in the territory in which the family lives' (*AL,* 290).

Conclusion

God has big and beautiful dreams for every person born and for the families into which they are born. These dreams are the result of his love for us, his children. To ensure that these dreams are fulfilled in the beautiful everyday of family life and in the wonderful tenderness that exists at the heart of family relationships, families need to be supported in very practical ways, particularly in terms of what Pope Francis says about the education of children. To do this, the Church must herself become a 'family of families' with all the qualities suggested above. Joy, tenderness and an awareness of the God of Love moving among us need to be what makes our parishes, as well as our families, come alive in Love.

Reflection Questions

1. Where in the 'beautiful ordinary' of your own family life do you see the God of Love?

2. How good are you at being attuned to what your family life teaches you about God? What would help you become more attuned to the God of Love at the heart of your family?

3. What is the challenge of 'patient realism' currently for you in your own family context?

4. How serious is the 'technological disconnect' Pope Francis writes about in chapter seven? What, in your view, needs to be done by families to address this problem?

5. How might parishes better support parents to educate their children in faith?

Endnotes

1. Leahy, B., *Dreaming Big: Living the Reality - Rediscovering Family Today,* Veritas Publications, August 2016

2. Conway, E., and Barry, C., *The Joy of Love: Love in the Family by Pope Francis – Study Guide to the Apostolic Exhortation,* Irish Catholic Ltd, 2016

3. Franchi, Leonardo. https://cvcomment.org/2016/05/11/how-amoris-laetitia-reclaims-the-role-of-family-in-education/

Chapter Eight
Accompanying, Discerning and Integrating Weakness

DONAL MURRAY

Chapter eight of *Amoris Laetitia*, opens with this statement:

> … although the Church realises that any breach of the marriage bond 'is against the will of God', she is also 'conscious of the frailty of many of her children'. (*AL*, 291)

That prompts a seemingly insoluble question. Can we balance the requirements of law and justice, which declare the marriage bond to be indissoluble, with the love and understanding that we should show to those whose lives breach that bond?

Take a familiar example of the balance between justice and mercy. When the prodigal son came home, the elder brother pointed out that he had given up all claim to be treated as one of the family when he left, taking everything to which he was entitled.

The father saw things differently. This young man was his son who had made a mess of his life. He continued to look at his son with the eyes of a loving father. So a person who had squandered his entire share of the family wealth was warmly received as a much loved son.

The elder brother's reaction was not unreasonable. 'Being patient does not mean letting ourselves be constantly mistreated' (*AL*, 92). The elder brother stood up for himself because he felt he was being put in a secondary position to make way for someone who no longer had any right to be there at all.

The point of the story, however, is that there is a bigger picture. As St John Paul II put it:

> ... mercy becomes an indispensable element in shaping
> mutual relationships ... It is impossible to establish
> this bond between people, if they wish to regulate their
> mutual relationships solely according to the measure
> of justice. In every sphere of interpersonal relationships
> justice must, so to speak, be 'corrected' to a considerable
> extent by that love which, as St Paul proclaims, 'is
> patient and kind' or, in other words, possesses the
> characteristics of that merciful love which is so much of
> the essence of the Gospel and Christianity.[1]

But laws are essential; we cannot flourish as individuals or as a society if we don't respect the law. The rights of individuals and the values that enable society to live as a human community need to be protected.

How can these two apparently contradictory, but essential, elements be reconciled in practice? That question runs through chapter eight of *Amoris Laetitia*. Pope Francis warns, quoting Pope Benedict, that no 'easy recipes' exist.[2]

Marriage is Indissoluble

The marriage promise is of its nature perpetual. Pope Francis puts it like this:

> Lovers do not see their relationship as merely
> temporary ... Those who witness the celebration of
> a loving union, however fragile, trust that it will pass
> the test of time. Children not only want their parents

to love one another, but also to be faithful and remain together. These and similar signs show that it is in the very nature of conjugal love to be definitive. The lasting union expressed by the marriage vows is more than a formality or a traditional formula; it is rooted in the natural inclinations of the human person. (*AL*, 123)

The teaching of the Church about the indissolubility of marriage should not be soft-pedalled:

… in no way must the Church desist from proposing the full ideal of marriage, God's plan in all its grandeur … A lukewarm attitude, any kind of relativism, or an undue reticence in proposing that ideal, would be a lack of fidelity to the Gospel and also of love on the part of the Church for young people themselves. (*AL*, 307)

The indissolubility of marriage is an eloquent expression of human dignity and freedom. Two people, usually young, stand before their family, their friends, their Church and their God and make the extraordinary promise that they will remain a faithful husband and wife to each other, 'for better for worse, for richer, for poorer, in sickness and in health', as long as they live. These are not empty words. The making of such a promise implies that human beings are capable of deciding what they will be to each other, whatever may happen. The courage of that commitment is what leads to the surreptitious dabbing of eyes at many a wedding. We are moved by the unconditional expression of commitment by a couple who usually have yet to experience how difficult life can be, but who can and do make a lifelong promise.

Any suggestion that this commitment need not 'really' be until death would not do justice to the depth and courage and nobility of the couple's promise. The Church's understanding of marriage proclaims that human beings are indeed capable of making, of meaning and of living that promise for the whole of their lives. Pope Francis said:

> When a man and a woman celebrate the sacrament of marriage, God, so to speak, 'reflects himself' in them, imprints on them his features and the indelible character of his love. Marriage is the icon of God's love for us.[3]

The most fundamental consequence of the teaching that marriage is indissoluble is that there cannot be a 'second marriage' as long as both partners to a valid sacramental marriage are alive. In no way does *Amoris Laetitia* weaken that teaching.

Being Merciful: Accompaniment

So where does that leave the second side our dilemma – namely mercy? It leads us to chapter eight: 'Accompanying, Discerning and Integrating Weakness'.

Amoris Laetitia, following in the footsteps of recent Popes,[4] stresses that people who are divorced and have married civilly should feel part of the Church. 'They are not excommunicated' and they should not be treated as such, since they remain part of the ecclesial community. (*AL*, 243) These situations 'require careful discernment and respectful accompaniment'. (*AL*, 243)

Pope Benedict said to those who have experienced breakdown: 'I encourage you to remain united to your communities, and I earnestly hope that your dioceses are developing suitable initiatives to welcome and accompany you.'[5]

People in difficult situations which are 'against the will of God', such as a breach of the marriage bond, should not feel excluded, but rather accompanied, by the Christian community. Thank God, in many cases, they have that support from families and friends, but they may feel, like many people whose lives are in different ways out of keeping with the teaching of the Church, that they are being judged and condemned. In the parable of the Pharisee and the tax collector, the person who was out of favour with God was the one who thought he was a paragon of virtue and who judged tax collectors to be outside the pale. God's judgement was very different (Lk 18:9-14). Cardinal Ratzinger said:

> The Pharisee no longer knows that he too has guilt.
> He has a completely clear conscience. But this silence
> of conscience makes him impenetrable to God and
> humanity, while the cry of conscience which plagues the
> tax collector makes him capable of truth and love.[6]

Only the person who knows his or her need of mercy can understand what mercy means. That is central to *Amoris Laetitia*:

> It is a matter of reaching out to everyone, of needing
> to help each person find his or her proper way of
> participating in the ecclesial community and thus
> to experience being touched by an 'unmerited,
> unconditional and gratuitous' mercy. No one can be
> condemned for ever, because that is not the logic of the
> Gospel! Here I am not speaking only of the divorced
> and re-married, but of everyone, in whatever situation
> they find themselves. (*AL*, 297)

We are never in a position to judge another person. We are repeatedly told that Pope Francis asked, 'who am I to judge?' But that that's not quite what he said. The official translation said: 'who am I to judge *him?*' An irresistible instinct removed what is now seen as the exclusive word, 'him', so we were left with 'who am I to judge?' The full sentence in the original Italian[7] would be more correctly translated as, 'If a person is gay and seeks the Lord and has good will, then who am I to judge that person (or to judge such a person)?' It may sound like a quibble, but the difference is crucial. What the Pope said was not who am I to say that someone's ideas or actions are wrong or mistaken, but 'who am I to *judge a person.*'[8]

The difference between judging a person and judging the person's actions or opinions is vital. To say 'I don't agree with your position' is not the same as saying, 'I don't respect you'. If it was, civilised discussion would be impossible. After all, I may find myself disagreeing with my own ideas, because at a later date, I look back and think: 'the way I saw it then was wrong'.

We can never judge *a person.* A person's heart is beyond the grasp of others, or even of him/herself.[9] In the past, the situation of people who divorced after a valid sacramental marriage and entered a new union, was often described as 'living in a state of mortal sin'. If that were an accurate description, the question of receiving the Eucharist while in that state would be a clear negative. The proper meaning of mortal sin is that it destroys the person's relationship with God; it is mortal, or lethal, to that relationship. A 'state of mortal sin' would mean that a person's relationship with God was not just damaged, but broken.

The term 'mortal sin', correctly understood, cannot be identified with a particular action. To say, as we often did, 'missing Mass on Sunday is a mortal sin' confuses two distinct things. An action may be clearly wrong, but its effect on the person's relationship with God depends on the degree of their freedom and their knowledge of how wrong their action was. A state of mortal sin is indeed possible for people through injustice, violence, hatred, dishonesty etc. Someone's life may be in serious and unrepentant conflict with the love that is God's gift. If so, they should not receive the Eucharist. But, the state of a person's relationship with God is never for us to judge.

Amoris Laetitia says:

> The Church possesses a solid body of reflection concerning mitigating factors and situations.[10] Hence it is can no longer simply be said that all those in any 'irregular' situation are living in a state of mortal sin and are deprived of sanctifying grace. (*AL*, 301)

Whatever people's situation, the Church's role is to be an instrument of God's mercy and to walk with all the members of Christ's Body, on their journey of life. Pope Francis said:

> I understand those who prefer a more rigorous pastoral care which leaves no room for confusion. But I sincerely believe that Jesus wants a Church attentive to the goodness which the Holy Spirit sows in the midst of human weakness, a Mother who, while clearly expressing her objective teaching, 'always does what good she can, even if in the process, her shoes get soiled by the mud of the street'. The Church's pastors, in proposing to the faithful the full ideal of the Gospel and the Church's teaching, must also help them to treat the weak with compassion, avoiding aggravation or unduly harsh or hasty judgements. (*AL*, 308)

Discernment

The second aspect of the response to these situations is what *Amoris Laetitia* calls 'careful discernment'. (*AL*, 243) Pope Francis is well aware that what he is saying could be misinterpreted in a way that would undermine the nature of marriage as indissoluble. He stresses that he is not talking about a free-for-all, but about a careful and honest looking at the truth of one's situation. In practice that requires accompaniment by someone who will help to find the truth while avoiding 'judgements which do not take account of the complexity of various situations':

> It is a matter of reaching out to everyone, of needing
> to help each person find his or her proper way of
> participating in the ecclesial community and thus
> to experience being touched by an 'unmerited,
> unconditional and gratuitous' mercy. No one can be
> condemned for ever, because that is not the logic of the
> Gospel! Here I am not speaking only of the divorced
> and re-married, but of everyone, in whatever situation
> they find themselves (cf. Mt 18:17). (*AL*, 296, 297)

The document strongly upholds the doctrine of indissolubility but also looks at the pastoral care of people in situations which are not in keeping with the Church's teaching: 'To show understanding in the face of exceptional situations never implies[11] dimming the light of the fuller ideal, or proposing less than what Jesus offers to the human being'. (*AL*, 307)

Saint John Paul made some important points in this regard. He wrote in *Familiaris Consortio* about what he called 'gradualness'. God's law is true and is good for humanity. We do not, however, come to recognise God's law fully and live it wholeheartedly all at once. Growth in understanding and living

God's plan would be hindered rather than advanced by watering down the truth – God's law is the path to the salvation for which human hearts are restless.

> What is needed is a continuous, permanent conversion which, while requiring an interior detachment from every evil and an adherence to good in its fullness, is brought about concretely in steps which lead us ever forward.[12]

This assumes that the couple, in seeking to discern their situation are willing to accept the Church's vision of the sacrament of marriage, its indissolubility and its meaning as the icon of God's faithful love.

What options, then, are open to people in a second union which cannot be a sacramental marriage? In the past we would simply have said, they should either abandon the relationship, or live without any sexual relationship. Sometimes, that may be the right solution. However, Pope Francis recognises that it is not always so simple. There are for instance long standing second unions of mutual fidelity where the best interests of children must be considered. While conscious that their situation is out of keeping with the Church's vision of marriage, the couple face 'the great difficulty of going back without feeling in conscience that one would fall into new sins'. *Amoris Laetitia* acknowledges situations 'where, for serious reasons, such as the children's upbringing, a man and woman cannot satisfy the obligation to separate' (*AL*, 298, *GS*, 51). What Pope Francis is raising here is a new issue, namely that in some situations a couple may see no morally right way of rectifying their situation: any possible route they can take seems to be wrong. Where such cases exist, we cannot conclude that the partners are trapped in a state of sin with no way out. 'No one can be condemned for ever.' (*AL*, 297)

There are also the cases such as, 'those who have entered into a second union for the sake of the children's upbringing, and are sometimes subjectively certain in conscience that their previous and irreparably broken marriage had never been valid' (*AL*, 298).

That conscientious conviction may be correct. They may have submitted the case to a marriage tribunal, a path which Pope Francis has made more accessible and less complicated.[13] However, the tribunal may say that there is no proof the marriage was null – which is not the same as proof that it was not null. It is possible, for instance, that important witnesses are unable or unwilling to participate. It is also possible that the evidence cannot be interpreted with any certainty. Then there is the question as to whether the parties had sufficiently mature faith for an adequate understanding and acceptance of the meaning of marriage as a sacrament.

Pope Francis understands that many people would like things to be clearer through 'a more rigorous pastoral care which leaves no room for confusion' (*AL*, 308). Saint John Paul, for instance, said: 'the Church reaffirms her practice, which is based upon Sacred Scripture, of not admitting to Eucharistic Communion divorced persons who have remarried'.[14] While standing firm about indissolubility and the impossibility of a second marriage, Pope Francis does not repeat that position. *Amoris Laetitia* says: 'neither the Synod nor this Exhortation could be expected to provide a new set of general rules, canonical in nature and applicable to all cases' (*AL*, 300).

But he does suggest some of the searching questions that an honest discernment needs to face:

> … how did they act towards their children when the conjugal union entered into crisis; whether or not they made attempts at reconciliation; what has become

of the abandoned party; what consequences the new relationship has on the rest of the family and the community of the faithful; and what example is being set for young people who are preparing for marriage ...

What we are speaking of is a process of accompaniment and discernment which 'guides the faithful to an awareness of their situation before God. Conversation with the priest, in the internal forum, contributes to the formation of a correct judgment on what hinders the possibility of a fuller participation in the life of the Church and on what steps can foster it and make it grow.[15]

This requires:

... humility, discretion and love for the Church and her teaching, in a sincere search for God's will and a desire to make a more perfect response to it". ... When a responsible and tactful person, who does not presume to put his or her own desires ahead of the common good of the Church, meets with a pastor capable of acknowledging the seriousness of the matter before him, there can be no risk that a specific discernment may lead people to think that the Church maintains a double standard. (*AL*, 300)

This is a call to enter into a mature and honest discernment. That is something we are not used to, and we should not underestimate the challenge it represents.

A legalistic attitude only wants to know 'is there a law against it?' and concludes that 'so long as there is no definite rule, I can to what I wish'.[16] But conscience is not just a mechanism to decide what the law says. It seeks to respond to the truth which lies deep within us because, at the first moment of our existence, God invited us to share in the truth and in the divine life.[17] That cannot be reduced simply to obeying rules.

Once in a survey on pastoral issues, a query came back from one group – 'What does the bishop want us to say?' A similar response to *Amoris Laetitia* would ask, 'Why doesn't the Pope just tell us what to do?' Pope Francis doesn't do that, not least because not every question can be answered from outside the real situation of those involved in it. More importantly, he wants to encourage the honest, painful discernment which does not simply seek a ready-made answer, but seeks the encounter with Jesus Christ, the Way, Truth and Life, which is the heart of Christianity.[18]

Integrating Weakness

Chapter eight asks how the Church can integrate into its life people who, at least at present, cannot regularise their situation.

It is not enough to say to a couple, 'your situation is against the will of God, when you change it we can reach out and welcome you'. The community of the baptised should receive them as members of the family, walk with them and care for them in their efforts to understand and to do what is right however complex their situation. That is a task not only for pastors but for the whole community in whose name they were 'welcomed with great joy' at their Baptism.

> Naturally, every effort should be made to encourage the development of an enlightened conscience, formed and guided by the responsible and serious discernment of one's pastor, and to encourage an ever greater trust in

God's grace. Yet conscience can do more than recognise that a given situation does not correspond objectively to the overall demands of the Gospel. It can also recognise with sincerity and honesty what for now is the most generous response which can be given to God, and come to see with a certain moral security that it is what God himself is asking amid the concrete complexity of one's limits, while yet not fully the objective ideal.(*AL*, 303)

Some people hoped for clear rules. On the day *Amoris Laetitia* was published Cardinal Schönborn said: "They will be disappointed. The Pope says: 'What is possible is simply "a renewed encouragement to undertake a responsible personal and pastoral discernment of particular cases"'. (*AL*, 300) [19]

The final words of the Code of Canon Law say that the supreme law for the Church is always the salvation of souls.[20] The purpose of the Church is not to condemn people but to lead them into a deeper relationship with God,[21] 'not to condemn the world but to save it'.[22]

The *Catechism of the Catholic Church* says of the Ten Commandments: 'The Commandments, properly so called, come in the second place; they express the implications of belonging to God through the establishment of the covenant'.[23]

Jesus says of the commandments to love God and our neighbour, 'On these two commandments hang *all the law* and the prophets' (Mt 22:40).

The rules are important, but there is a more fundamental law which is the deepest meaning of the rules. Saint Thomas Aquinas says: 'even the letter of the Gospel could kill if the saving grace of faith were not present within'.[24] Too often the Church is seen primarily as a purveyor of rules rather than as the sign and instrument of the mystery of God's infinitely merciful love. What that love asks of us has to be discovered in honest and often painful discernment.

Law and pastoral concern are not opposed concepts: 'The love of truth is the fundamental point of encounter between law and pastoral concern.'[25]

Everything should to be done in the light of the striking words of St John Paul:

> The Church lives an authentic life when she professes
> and proclaims mercy – the most stupendous attribute of
> the Creator and of the Redeemer – and when she brings
> people close to the sources of the Saviour's mercy, of
> which she is the trustee and dispenser.[26]

Reflection Questions

1. 'The most fundamental consequence of the teaching that marriage is indissoluble is that there cannot be a 'second marriage' as long as both partners to a valid sacramental marriage are alive. In no way does *Amoris Laetitia* weaken that teaching.' Is this a counter-cultural message in the world we live in today?

2. People who are in so-called irregular situations should not be excluded from parish life. As Pope Benedict says: 'I encourage you to remain united to your communities, and I earnestly hope that your dioceses are developing suitable initiatives to welcome and accompany you'. Are couples in difficult situations aware of this emphasis? How could it be communicated at parish level?

3. 'The difference between judging a person and judging the person's actions or opinions is vital.' Where in your own life have you seen the importance of this distinction?

4. 'This is a call to enter into a mature and honest discernment. That is something we are not used to, and we should not underestimate the challenge it represents.' In the context of chapter eight, what are some of these challenges?

Endnotes

1. John Paul II, *Dives in Misericordia*, 14
2. Benedict XVI, Address to World Meeting of Families, Milan, 2 June 2012; (AL, 298)
3. Pope Francis, General Audience, 2 April 2014; *AL*, 121
4. Cf. John Paul 11, *Familiaris Consortio*, 84
5. Benedict XVI *Homily at the World Meeting of Families*, Milan, 3 June 2012

6. Ratzinger, J., *Conscience and Truth*, Presentation to US Bishops, Dallas, February 1991
7. Se una persona è gay e cerca il Signore e ha buona volontà, ma chi sono io per giudicarla?
8. For a fuller treatment, see Murray, Donal, *In a Landscape Redrawn*, Veritas, 2017, p. 61ff.
9. Cf. *Catechism of the Catholic Church*, 2563
10. Cf. *Catechism of the Catholic Church*, 1856–1862
11. Merriam Webster 'imply' – to involve by necessary consequence
12. John Paul II, *Familiaris Consortio*, [FC]
13. Cf. Francis, *Mitis Judex*, cf. *AL*, 244
14. *FC*, 84
15. *AL*, 300 cf. also *Relatio Finalis*, Synod of Bishops, 24 October 2015
16. Ratzinger Cf. *Conscience and Truth*, 1
17. Cf. *Gaudium et Spes*, 19
18. Benedict XVI, *Deus Caritas Est*, 1
19. Schönborn, C., at the launch of *Amoris Laetitia*, 8 April 2016
20. *Code of Canon Law, Can.* 1752
21. Cf. John Paul II, *Mulieris Dignitatem*, 27n
22. Cf. John 3:17
23. *Catechism of the Catholic Church*, 2062
24. Aquinas, *Summa Theologiae*, I-II q.106 a.2c
25. Senèze, N., *la synodalité au coeur de l'exhortation*, La Croix, 6 April 2016 (my trans)
26. John Paul II, *Dives in Misericordia*, 13

Chapter Nine

The Spirituality of Marriage and the Family

PATRICK TREACY

The spirituality of marriage and the family is the title and content of the final chapter of *Amoris Laetitia*. It is the shortest chapter of nine in this text. It is also the culmination of the expression of the Christian understanding of marriage and the family with which the entire text is concerned.

While so many of us unconsciously live a spirituality of marriage and family life, its inspiring nature came to the forefront of our awareness in Ireland recently through the life of a remarkable family in Killaloe, County Clare. On Sunday, 16 October 2016, the late Munster rugby player, captain and head coach, Anthony Foley, died suddenly at the age of forty-two in a Paris hotel room. Later that day, the Munster team, which he was then coaching, were to play their opening match of the European Champions Cup season against the Parisian side Racing Metro 92. The match was immediately postponed.

Having been a highly accomplished sportsman from his youth, Anthony Foley was invited back to his former school, St Munchin's College, to give team talks before particularly big games. It was reported that he did not say a lot but when he did say something, it was short and to the point:

Look at the crest. Look at your teammates. Your team is like a family. Don't let them down. Don't criticise them. If you have a row, get over it and next day get back up again. Support them in the bad times if something goes wrong and celebrate when something goes right.[1]

After the return of his body to his home on Wednesday evening, he was buried following Requiem Mass on Friday, 21 October 2016. The life of this man, the strength and dignity of his wife, Olive, and the character of his two young sons, Tony and Dan and his whole family, had a profound effect on countless people who mourned his loss and witnessed his funeral.

On the day following the funeral, the Munster team then played what was now their opening match of this competition against Glasgow Warriors from Scotland. It was a highly charged and yet sad occasion at Thomond Park, Limerick, where the men whom he had coached played quite brilliantly and won the match by 38 points to 17. Some of the players openly cried before and after the game. When it was over, the players formed a circle in the middle of the pitch and were joined by Anthony's two sons. Together, they all sang an operatic song traditionally associated with Munster Rugby: 'Stand Up and Fight'.

Later that evening, eleven year old Tony, Anthony's eldest son, created an appeal on Facebook with the simple request that, for the eight Sundays from 30 October, people go to Mass and pray for deceased family and friends and for his father. That date, 30 October, would have been his father's forty-third birthday. The number eight was his father's jersey number and the eight Sundays would culminate at 'that special family time of year, Christmas.'

Ironically, on the same day Tony launched his appeal, the next World Meeting of Families, which will take place in Dublin in August 2018, was launched at St Patrick's College, Drumcondra, Dublin. This world meeting will seek to explain the teachings of Pope Francis in *Amoris Laetitia* and he himself may well be in attendance. During the entire week that preceded this launch, the courage, inspiration and integrity of Anthony Foley's family incomparably displayed the renewed awareness of family that we are being called by Pope Francis to have. The bravery and dignity of this family, in the face of immense loss and grief, illuminates the words of Pope Francis at the end of chapter nine of *Amoris Laetitia*: 'May we never lose heart because of our limitations, or ever stop seeking that fullness of love and communion which God holds out before us' (*AL*, 325).

By making the spirituality of marriage and the family the final and climactic statement of this apostolic exhortation, Pope Francis is saying to all those committed to Catholicism and to the broader Christian family that the family home must be rediscovered as a primary place of the Church and of experiencing a real and lived presence of the persons of the Holy Trinity in our lives. Indeed, Pope Francis has gone so far as to suggest that what have been understood as ecclesial communities, that is communities of priests and those in religious life, need to model themselves upon the family. In his address after the Angelus in Saint Peter's Square on 31 May 2015, he said:

> … we have been entrusted with the task of edifying
> ecclesial communities which increasingly become
> families, capable of reflecting the splendour of the
> Trinity and evangelising not only with the words but
> with the power of the love of God that lives within us.

This theological idea of the family reflecting the splendour of the Holy Trinity is precisely reiterated by Pope Francis in *Amoris Laetitia*. He says:

> The triune God is a communion of love, and the family
> is its living reflection. (*AL*, 11)

In making this statement, Pope Francis proceeds in the same paragraph to refer to Saint John Paul II, whom he says shed light on this when he said, 'Our God in his deepest mystery is not solitude, but a family, for he has within himself fatherhood, sonship and the essence of the family, which is love. That love, in the divine family, is the Holy Spirit' (*AL*, 11).[2]

Pope Francis is signaling an important change of emphasis through the location of the spiritual significance of marriage and the family in their ultimate source – the persons of the Holy Trinity. It implies a much greater intimacy of a family with God and of the crucial role of the Christian household (referred to in Church documents as 'the domestic Church') in incarnating this in our lives and in the world. In other words, it is not simply that God is present in the world and that we are called to reflect this presence through the household but rather that by being one in a physical home, we are also one in a spiritual home with the persons of the Holy Trinity. In this spiritual home, God dwells within us and we dwell within God. The domestic Church moves from being seen solely as a physical place for Christian witness to also being included and transcended into a deeper mystical understanding of it as an icon of the household of each of us in God and of God's holding within each of us.

There are two particular sentences in the Old Testament which support the spirituality of the domestic church which Pope Francis is leading us into. In the book of Joshua, he says to the people: 'As for me and my household, we will serve the Lord' (Josh 24:15). This public pronouncement reflects the conventional understanding of the household as a place of witness to God and service of His will. In Psalm 23, however, the deeper spiritual significances of the Christian household are reflected in the words of the Psalmist: 'I shall dwell in the house of the Lord my whole life long' (Ps 23:6). It is this second understanding which also finds expression in the heart of the Gospel of John, as the most mystical of the Gospels. Jesus says: 'As the Father has loved me, so I have loved you. Abide in my love' (Jn 15:9). The invitation to abide in the love of God is to dwell in this love, to live within the holding environment of the love of God. It evokes the image of a dwelling place where one feels safe, secure and affirmed. This is re-iterated by Jesus when he says: 'If anyone loves me, he will obey my teaching. My Father will love him and we will come to him and make our home with him' (Jn 14:23).

This expression by Jesus of both he and his father making their home with us implies that they manifest themselves to us in no temporary way but that it is the privilege of Christians to enjoy their presence continually. They take up their residence in the heart of each one of us as their dwelling place, as a temple fit for their abode, a theme repeatedly taken up by St Paul in his letters to the Corinthians (cf. 1 Corinthians 3:16 'You are the temple of God'; 1 Corinthians 6:19; 'Your body is the temple of the Holy Spirit'; 2 Corinthians 6:16 'You are the temple of the living God.') In turn, we are called to live in their domain, their *domus*, their spiritual home, by being quietly, calmly confident of their eternal presence in the field of time and space in which we live and move and have our being.

Previously, it has been widely understood in Christian spirituality that the way of contemplation was the primary, if not even the exclusive way in which one could aspire to an experience of the mystical love of God. At the conclusion and climax of this apostolic exhortation, however, Pope Francis is saying something quite radically different and new. It is also something that someone who lives in a loving, permanent household has known all along: being immersed in the life of a household rooted in the love of God is to be immersed in God.

Such a household is not simply witnessing the presence of God to the world but the *milieu* of God within the world and the holding environment for the care of the presence of God in our own hearts.

Nonetheless, there is a danger in stressing this pivotal insight of Pope Francis that his expression of the mystical beauty of marriage and family life in some way occludes the calling of the family to go out into the world and to embrace all others with its own hospitality. Such an occlusion would obviously be entirely contrary to the general exhortations of Pope Francis that the Church goes to the peripheries and becomes a 'field hospital' for those who are in need of care and love. The deeper we are led into an interior knowledge of God, the more we are prompted to reach out to others, to become less self-absorbed and more sensitive and responsive to the human fragility which we all share.

Accordingly, Pope Francis also states in this chapter that the family 'has always been the nearest "hospital"'. He says that God's love is proclaimed 'through the living and concrete word whereby a man and the woman express their conjugal love' and that the two are thus mutual reflections of that divine love which comforts with a word, a look, a helping hand, a caress, an embrace. (*AL,* 321). All family life is described by him as 'a shepherding in mercy'. When a family is welcoming and reaches out to others, especially the poor and the neglected, Pope Francis says that it is 'a symbol, witness and participant in the Church's motherhood'. Social love, as a reflection of the Trinity, is what truly unifies the spiritual meaning of the family and its mission to others. He states:

> The family lives its spirituality precisely by being at one and the same time a domestic church and a vital cell for transforming the world. (*AL,* 324)

Just as Pope Francis focuses upon the inner and outer dimensions of family life, the mystical and the social, the inhalation and the exhalation of the breath of familial hospitality, he also ends this chapter by returning to a central teaching of his pontificate: that the mercy of God is found in the truthful acknowledgment of one's fragility. He concludes this chapter by explaining how this applies to families. He affirms that no family drops down from heaven perfectly formed and that families need constantly to grow and mature in the ability to love. Our contemplation of the fulfillment, which we have yet to attain, allows us to see in proper perspective the historical journey which we make as families.

The publication of *Amoris Laetitia* has given my wife and myself much to reflect upon. We were married in December 1998 and have had the great fortune to have four children who seem reasonably happy given the balance of their mother and notwithstanding the eccentricities of their father. In 2000, my wife Linda and myself started a domestic centre of Christian spirituality in our home, known as *Integritas*.[3] The purpose of this centre is to explore how the beauty, truth and goodness of Christian faith can be made more real through the domestic church. Through what has taken place here, it has become clearer that the domestic church is called to be a place that has nine qualities.

These nine qualities of the domestic Church are to be a place of prayer, a place of physical and mental well-being, a place founded upon the vow of marriage between a man and a woman, a place that respects the fundamental need of a child to be loved by a mother and a father, a place of fidelity to the local and universal Church, a place of education in Christian faith, a place that respects rights and responsibilities, a place that seeks to give something to society and finally, a place of ecumenical

Christian hospitality. The centre at Integritas seeks to grow into being such a place through regular prayer, holding classes on Christian spiritual themes, having conferences where certain concerns of the Church can be explored in a private setting and by publishing related materials. The underlying objective for all of this is to allow a domestic Church to become identifiable and to express an ecumenical Christian spirituality, which is rooted in marriage and family life, speaks about Christian faith in a way that is attractive and is an accurate response to the times we live in. Accordingly, at the core of this particular attempt to be a domestic Church is ecumenism. My wife is a member of the Church of Ireland as is our daughter. I am a member of the Roman Catholic Church as are our three sons.

In our experience, the key to the building of a domestic Church is a proper understanding of space. Firstly, the home must care for the family and its space is the priority. If the children have the space to be themselves and are given the freedom to engage or not engage in prayer or organised events as they wish, the whole enterprise can then grow together. In any event, children can often imbibe a greater sense of Christian faith indirectly. By this I mean that when people visit us and we have a meal together, they get a sense of faith from the lives of these people by simply being with them. Faith can often best be passed on to children if they see it being lived by others and have the opportunity to be with these people, to interact with them and to question and even challenge their beliefs. I welcome this as well as it often seems that only my beliefs are challenged by my children in our home. As the cross-examination becomes extended to others who stay with us, I will be increasingly relieved.

Secondly, it is of great value when the home (and if possible, a garden) remembers the presence of God in how it is designed, in the art or images displayed in the house and in the availability of books and literature about spiritual matters within it. Modern secularist culture, in all of its forms of media, contrives to make family homes fall into a state of forgetfulness about God. The presence of icons, for instance, in a house, is a powerful way of remembering God's presence and they are drawn upon in our own home. A prayer room, or a space within a room, that is devoted exclusively for prayer, also grounds the whole home spiritually and cultivates an atmosphere in all of it. As children live so much now with screens and in an intangible world, these physical ways of making space for God in the home are especially valuable for their spiritual development in our culture.

Finally, it is essential to make space in the time of the family home for God. A regular time for prayer, whether or not the children participate, sends a certain message to them that their parents believe in a reality beyond that which we encounter in daily life. When a child sees his or her parents at prayer, this must surely be a powerful communication of the importance of faith. Reading a book about God with a child, which is attractively presented, is an essential way of communicating faith, although in our family I have tended to buy the books and my wife has read them with the children. This has arisen because I have had a tendency to go off script, although my wife may have a different explanation.

The making of space for God in these varied ways in the home has one underlying objective which, incidentally, can never be realised by meditation or in practices such as mindfulness and which is essential for passing on faith to a child. It is to tell them the story of God and, in particular, the life of Jesus Christ. They must hear the story if we are to pass on to them the incomparable richness of the Judeo-Christian revelation which is the whole foundation of the society in which they live and will be educated in.

The name Integritas, for the domestic centre of Christian spirituality at our home, comes from the Latin for integrity. It refers to what is suggested to be at the heart of Christianity – that God seeks to draw all of His children back to Himself, to gather all of us into one (cf. Jn 17:21-23). At the centre of this plan is marriage between man and woman and the children that may come from them. The Christian understanding of marriage and family is where the divine plan of drawing all into the love of God finds its central locus for it is from our own parents that each of us, at our most vulnerable, are most open to the experience of the love of God. The protection of the integrity of marriage based upon the complementarity of man and woman is, therefore, at the foundation of Christian belief and of the well-being of society, a truth expressed by Pope Francis throughout *Amoris Laetitia* (cf. *AL, 52*).

As my wife and I also have a background in law, this centre became involved in the redefinition of marriage referendum that occurred in the Republic of Ireland in 2015. It sought to argue that the truthful resolution of this issue would be to give same-sex unions full recognition in our Constitution but not to alter the Christian understanding of marriage in Irish law, which heretofore had always been based upon the complementarity of man and woman. Instead, our nation rejected this and ratified our constitution, now saying that marriage is the foundation of the family and yet has nothing to do with the distinction between man and woman.[4]

The prophetic nature of Pope Francis' choice of Dublin for the next World Meeting of Families holds a mirror before us of the extent to which our country, in 2015, on the eve of the centenary of the Easter Rising, set its legal definition of the human person and the family completely against the Christian, biblical and natural law understanding of them. In particular, the way in which the family is now expressed in the law of the Republic of Ireland is totally contrary to the understanding of the human ecology of the family as intimated by Pope Francis in his encyclical *Laudato Si'* and then explained more explicitly in *Amoris Laetitia*.[5] What happened in the Republic of Ireland in 2015 is precisely identified in *Amoris Laetitia* where Pope Francis says:

> Many countries are witnessing a legal deconstruction of the family, tending to adopt models based almost exclusively on the autonomy of the individual will. (*AL*, 53)

I wish to end by noting this radical separation that was effected in the civil law of the Republic of Ireland in 2015 between the Christian understanding of marriage and the family and that which is now reflected in its constitution for this reason. We need to become aware of the importance now and in the years ahead, of married men and woman, their children and their relatives, visibly living in accordance with the integrity of the Christian understanding of marriage and the human ecology of the family. By doing so in our society, it will vitally assist in helping a balance to be struck between realising that no family reaches the ideal but also acknowledging that there is an ideal based on the complementarity of man and woman.

The challenge is to promote this ideal in a way which is inviting to others, rather than alienating. Our own deeply held convictions must spur us to the greatest courtesy and kindness in the way that we approach others. There can be no triumphalism, only a humble approach that is conscious of our own weaknesses. Conscious that every family is fragile, complicated and conflicted in endless ways, we also need to be confident that in the vowed covenant of marital love between a man and a woman and in the daily tasks of giving a child the best that a father and a mother can give, something of real and incomparable value is incarnated in the world. This reality can be deconstructed in our laws but it cannot ever be devalued in its beauty, truth and goodness. It is the importance of living in accordance with the Christian understanding of marriage and the family, particularly when it is rejected by our civil laws, that makes the emergence of 'the domestic Church' a central locus for the future witness of Christian faith. The domestic church, founded upon the marriage of a man and a woman and the parenting of children by a mother and a father, is an ideal which, when lived with integrity, is the foundation of human development and the good of society. It offers a renewed understanding of Christian education, the basis for a principled society and a truly ecumenical future for all Christians in one family.

The statement of this ideal is not to deny that the Christian spirituality of marriage and the family must emanate from lived experience, with all of the human limitations and woundedness inherent in this. In *Amoris Laetitia*, Pope Francis, therefore, urges us to always start with the reality of where we are in marriage and in family life but to also keep in mind the ideal of our end in the Kingdom of God. He says:

> All of us are called to keep striving towards something greater than ourselves and our families, and every family must feel this constant impulse. Let us make this journey as families, let us keep walking together. What we have been promised is greater than we can imagine. May we never lose heart because of our limitations, or ever stop seeking that fullness of love and communion which God holds out before us. (*AL,* 325)

This ideal is to be fully with God, who loves us and whose mercy and care for us are endless. Pope Francis urges us to have faith in this. For this to happen, we are truly assisted by seeing this faith in the actions of other families, such as that exemplified in 2016 by an eleven year old boy, his remarkable family and their friends in Killaloe, County Clare.

Reflection Questions

1. Tony Foley's appeal had a perceptible impact on attendance at Mass in Limerick, according to some priests of the diocese. The final Mass in the campaign was celebrated at the Knock Shrine by parish priest Fr Richard Gibbons and thousands attended. Is there a possibility that people have drifted away rather than chosen to move away from mass attendance? Does it take a tragedy to remind us of its importance?

2. 'Being immersed in the life of a household rooted in the love of God is to be immersed in God.' What does this statement mean to you?

3. Integritas has a highly developed programme of prayer, spirituality and welcome. Are there aspects of the model that can be applied in every household?

4. When it comes to controversial issues such as same-sex marriage, how can believers best respect the spirit of Pope Francis' words?

Endnotes

1. *The Irish Times*, Gerry Thornley, Saturday 22 October 2016, Sports Supplement, p. 3
2. This was said by St John Paul II in the course of his homily at the Eucharistic Celebration in Puebla de los Ángeles on 28 January 1979
3. Integritas, a domestic centre of Christian spirituality, Ennisnag, Stoneyford, Co. Kilkenny, Ireland R95 CR7W (www.integritas.ie and e-mail: enquiries@integritas.ie)

4. This contradiction at the centre of Article 41 of the Constitution of Ireland (which provides for 'The Family' in Irish law) is seen clearly when one contrasts Article 41.3.1 with the newly inserted Article 41.4. The former states that 'The State pledges itself to guard with special care the institution of Marriage, on which the Family is founded, and to protect it against attack'. The latter states that 'Marriage may be contracted in accordance with law by two persons without distinction as to their sex'.

5. This legal edifice is constructed upon Article 41.4 of the Constitution of Ireland which then supports the provisions of the Children and Family Relationships Act, the Gender Recognition Act and the Marriage Act, all of which were enacted in the Republic of Ireland in 2015.

About the Contributors

Brendan Leahy is the Catholic Bishop of Limerick. Prior to his episcopal ordination, he taught Theology at St Patrick's College, Maynooth, Mater Dei Institute of Education and Clonliffe College, Dublin. He is the author of numerous publications.

Bairbre Cahill is married to Danny and is mother to Caoimhe, Deirbhile, Méabh and Diarmuid. Bairbre has degrees in Psychology and Theology, and has a particular interest in the spirituality of family life and the sacramentality of the everyday. She also writes a regular column for *The Irish Catholic* and has published three books with Redemptorist Publications including *Living with grief – walking the spiral.*

Elizabeth and Frank Reynolds have been married for thirty-four years; they have two sons, now in their early twenties. They live in Coleraine and both work as librarians. Elizabeth and Frank have over twenty years experience working with ACCORD as relationship counsellors.

Breda O'Brien is a columnist with *The Irish Times*, and *The Irish Catholic*. She is a second-level teacher and frequent contributor to media debates on social, religious, ethical and education issues. Married to Brendan Conroy, she has four children. In the past, she has worked as a columnist with the *Sunday Business Post*, as a researcher in RTÈ, and as a video producer. She has a degree in Theology and English from the Mater Dei Institute, Dublin, and a Masters in Communication, from Dublin City University.

Fr Frankie Murray was ordained for the Diocese of Ardagh and Clonmacnoise in 1977. He was the Diocesian Advisor for schools. He then served in the Cathedral parish of Longford, in Ferbane and now in Drumshanbo where he is parish priest.

He is very committed to CASA which is a Caring and Sharing Association supporting people with disabilities. He speaks with passion about the profound gift those with a disability are to our church; he often reminds us how these gifted people can lead us to a place of the heart that is the home of compassion.

Deirdre O' Rawe is Director of ACCORD, Northern Ireland. She studied Social Policy and Social Administration at UCD and undertook postgraduate studies in management at QUB. She is currently studying pastoral theology at St Patrick's Pontifical University, Maynooth. She is a native of Fermanagh and past pupil of Mount Lourdes Grammar School, Enniskillen. She and her husband live in Belfast with their two sons.

Kate Liffey is a Religious Educator. She is a graduate of Mater Dei Institute of Education (Dublin) and is currently working for the Council for Catechetics of the Irish Bishops' Conference. She is married to Geoff and has two daughters and one son.

Bishop Donal Murray lectured in Moral Theology in Mater Dei Institute and in Holy Cross College from 1969 to 1982. He was Auxiliary Bishop of Dublin from 1982 to 1996 and then Bishop of Limerick until 2009. Though now retired, he continues to be involved in issues of ecumenism, bioethics and education. His most recent publication is *In a Landscape Redrawn* (Veritas 2017).

Patrick Treacy is married with four children. He is a Senior Counsel. Together with his wife, Linda Rainsberry, they facilitate a domestic centre of Christian spirituality at their home in County Kilkenny (www.integritas.ie). He has written a text in anticipation of the World Meeting of Families in Dublin in 2018 entitled 'Mission Territory – Pope Francis, Ireland and the World Meeting of Families 2018' and a copy of it can be downloaded from this website by clicking on to 'Ireland and the World Meeting of Families 2018' on its homepage.